THE M.

THE

SCRIPTURAL DOCTRINE

OF THE

TRINITY,

INVESTIGATED AND DEFENDED.

BY M. W. ALFORD.

The grace of the Lord Jesus Christ, and the love of God, and the communion of the Holy Ghost, be with you all. Amen.—*Paul.*

DOVER, N. H.

PUBLISHED BY THE TRUSTEES OF THE FREEWILL BAPTIST CONNECTION.

William Burr, Printer.

1842.

Entered according to Act of Congress, in the year 1842, by
WM. BURR, Agent of " the Trustees of the F. W. B. Connection," in the Clerk's Office of the District Court of New Hamp-
shire.

PREFACE.

Few subjects have been more fully or ably discussed than the one examined in the following pages. Still the writer feels warranted in calling the attention of the public to it again, from various considerations. While truth is forever the same, and immutable, error is ever assuming new and specious forms. It therefore becomes necessary, frequently, to trace it in its tergiversations, and expose its insidious devices in order to protect community from imposition. The error we here oppose, is as changeable in its aspect as the chameleon. Arianism, Socinianism, Unitarianism, Rationalism, and Neology, are the leading titles, under which it has presented itself to the world. But it has not always been honest enough to sail under its own colors; but has frequently sought to make even the sacred name of Christ sanction its abominations. Under the garb of piety, it has insinuated itself into the church, and led astray some of the sincere followers of the Savior. We would especially beseech such to investigate this subject diligently, and see that the doctrines of men are not received as the teachings of the Holy Spirit. Let such beware how they countenance a doctrine that strikes at the vitals of Christianity. If, as the writer believes, the error in question is one of the most pernicious errors ever devised, then it is the duty of every one to be thoroughly informed respecting it. Having been called to the examination of this subject, both in public and private, and to witness the various measures it adopts for its propagation, the author has thought proper to present, briefly, the result of his investigations to the public, in the following pages. And if this little work shall be instrumental of leading any out of error into truth, or of making the truth appear more precious to those who have already embraced it, his object will be accomplished. All he would ask of the reader in relation to this production, is, a careful and impartial examination; believing assuredly that truth will ultimately prevail, which is his constant prayer.

M. W. A.

Byron, N. Y. May, 1842.

THE MANUAL.

WHILE contemplating the character of the Infinite, Uncreated, Invisible, Immortal, Incomprehensible, BEING ; we are at once filled with feelings of deep solemnity and reverential delight.

While we view his awful majesty—his jealousy for his own holiness—his utter abhorrence of all sin—his dreadful wrath, we can but be solemnly impressed.

But while we consider his love in giving his Son —the condescension of the Son in suffering, bleeding, groaning and dying to redeem us from sin ; who can but feel his heart melt with emotions of tenderness and delight? While we reflect on the vast consequences involved in the subject before us, we trust that the Holy Spirit will grant us aid to arrive at the truth in all our conclusions.

CHAPTER I.

Evidences of the real humanity of our Lord Jesus Christ. His body was human—He had a human soul.

IT is an evident fact that Christ our blessed Savior must have possessed two natures, or he did not.

He was human, that is, he possessed a human body and soul, or he did not.

Now, if Unitarianism be correct when it declares that Christ possessed but one nature, then it follows that that nature must have been a created nature in every sense of the term considered, or it was not.

I. Christ our Savior possessed a *human body*.

1. This is evident from the following passage. Phil. 2:7, 8. "But made himself of no reputation, and took upon him the form of a servant, and was made in the likeness of men, and being found in fashion as a man, he humbled himself, and became obedient unto death, even the death of the cross." From this, it is quite evident that he who was eternally with the Father took the *form of a man*.

2. This form or body was one in *all respects human*. Heb. 2:14—17. "For as much then as the children are partakers of flesh and blood, he also himself likewise took part of the same, that through death he might destroy him that had the power of death, that is, the devil; and deliver them who through fear of death were all their lifetime subject to bondage. For verily he took not on him the nature of angels; but he took on him the seed of Abraham. Wherefore in all things it behooved him to be made like unto his brethren, that he might be a merciful and faithful High Priest in things pertaining to God." If he was not possessed of a human body and soul, he was not in *all things* like his brethren. He participated in the *same nature* with

the rest of mankind, and in this respect He was as truly human as were the children who were also partakers of flesh and blood, for he partook, or took, part of the same nature which they inherently possessed.

He tells his disciples plainly after his resurrection what his body was. Luke 24:39. "Behold my hands and my feet, that it is I myself: handle me, and see, for a spirit hath not *flesh and bones* as ye see me have." Here then we have his own words for it, that his body was composed of *flesh and bones.* It seems to be almost trifling to attempt to prove that that flesh and those bones he mentioned were human! But such is the pertinacity with which many cling to errors, that it is almost indispensable to prove, that our Lord possessed human *flesh, blood, and bones.* *

* We wish the reader to bear in mind, in the outset, that Unitarians maintain the idea that Christ possessed but one nature, and that was all divine. This is the doctrine of that sect, who call themselves, "The Christian Church," or we will say, it is the doctrine of the leading ministers and members of that sect. Thus one of their writers has it :

"But to believe we do incline,
That Jesus Christ was all divine."

The reader will see in perusing this work, that we have cited some of their authors to prove this to be their leading sentiment. How completely this idea accords with one John speaks of, when he says ;—"Many deceivers are entered into the world, who confess not that *Jesus Christ is come in the flesh.* This is a deceiver and an anti-christ." 2 John, 7th verse. He who believes in a Savior that possesses "Divine flesh" must entertain strange notions of Divinity.

The common acceptation of the term *divinity*, is, "deity, divine

3. He was subject to the same laws that all his brethren were subject to. Luke 3:51. We find him subject to his parents. Gal. 4:4, 5. "God sent forth his Son, made of a woman, made under the law, to redeem them that were under the law." As a human being, it became him to be subject to the laws which recognize government and control human actions.

4. He had the susceptibilities of man.

(1.) Tempted by the devil. Matt. 4:1.

(2.) Fasted and was hungry. Mark 11:12. "And on the morrow, when they were come from Bethany, he was hungry."

(3.) He was thirsty. John 4:7. "Jesus saith unto her give me to drink." John 19:28. "Jesus knowing that all things were now accomplished that the Scriptures might be fulfilled, saith I thirst."

(4.) He was *fatigued* by his labors. John 4:6. "Jesus therefore being *weary* with his journey sat thus on the well."

(5.) He slept as a man. Matt. 8:24. While the sea was roaring, its waves dashing, and the tempest howling, he slept. But as soon as he was awaken-

nature," and we cannot possibly conceive that this nature could suffer and die. As we have stated in another place, so we would say here; angelic nature might have suffered, but could not have died. But if Christ possessed but one nature, and that was divine, or angelic, or if it was human, how could he say, " I have power to lay down my life, and I have power to take it again." If he possessed but one nature, and that was now dead, and incarcerate in the tomb, had it power of itself to rise and burst the bands of death? Suppose an angel could die, and be buried in the grave; has that angel power to take his life again? Assuredly not. Nor has any mere creature that power.

ed by his disciples, he rose, and at once, and with the voice of Omnipotence, hushed the headlong waves, and calmed the roaring winds. So there was a great calm.

(6.) He grieved, felt, and wept as a man. John 11:35. And was subject to pain and *death*. His body was not a spiritual body. Spirits cannot die. The spirit of man is immortal, and only the body is subject to mortality. His body was not of the nature of angels, for angelic nature cannot die. They have fallen and are still in being, wretched being indeed, but death is forever removed from them. But the body of Jesus died.

> " Well might the sun in darkness hide,
> And shut his glories in,
> When Christ the mighty Savior died,
> For man the creature's sin."

(7.) The angel, by the appointment of God, gave the most significant title to the Savior before his birth. He was to be called JESUS, because he was to save his people from their sins. But he was also to be called IM-MANU-EL, God with us. Of this being, it was said by Isaiah, that "Butter and honey he should eat," intimating that he should receive the same kind of nutriment that other men, or human beings, partook of, that he should be one WITH US, and at the same time GOD. Of him it is said, " He was made of a woman, made under the law, to redeem them that were under the law," and the first promise that alludes to him as the Savior, speaks of him as "The seed of the woman."

Gen. 3:15. He was God, made known, or manifested, in the flesh. From his name, *Immanuel*,
from the fact that he was the seed of the woman,
of the seed of Abraham, what other rational conclusion can be drawn, than that he possessed the nature of human beings? In this nature, God was
manifested to us, and this we term the incarnation
of the Deity. How Divinity was united with humanity we do not pretend to know; but we do know
that the Bible teaches this doctrine, and on the veracity
and validity of inspiration we most heartily believe
it.* Some have supposed his body was not human, because it is said that "God sent his Son in
the *likeness* of sinful flesh." But observe, "*in the
likeness of sinful flesh.*" His nature was perfectly
pure, but it had the likeness of ours, which is wholly corrupt. He was tempted in all points as we
are, yet without sin. Now the man who reads the
evidences of the human nature of our Savior, which
are so abundant in the volume of Life, and yet cannot see that the doctrine we are here advocating is

* The union of matter and mind in man is usually believed, but
the manner of that union we cannot define. We know this connection exists, and if we acknowledge it to be incomprehensible,
yet it is indisputably true. Nothing can be known of mind as a
separate entity, and the body without the mind is perfectly insen-
sible, yet the only medium through which the operations of the
mind are known to us is the body. We ask the man who rejects
the idea that Christ possessed *human* and *divine* natures united, because he cannot completely comprehend it, if he is not bound by
the same principle to reject the union of matter and mind in man?
Certainly so. But this is rejecting his senses and consciousness!
and denying what he knows to be true.

scriptural, must dwell in rare darkness. What proof could be possibly sufficient to establish this point, if it is yet unproved? Though Unitarians may reject or ridicule the idea of an incarnation of the Divine Being, yet we can scarcely see how inspiration can make the proof more pointed, or more conclusive.

But where and what is the evidence that Christ possessed but *one* nature? This is asserted over and over and again by Unitarians, but where is the proof? It is objected by Unitarians, that "the Bible does no where assert that Christ possesses two natures." The Bible no where asserts that one and one are two, yet we believe it. But the Bible asserts that Christ is *God*, and that he is *man*, and we know the nature of God is one nature, and the nature of man is another nature, and we call these, *two natures*; and as we find them both manifest in *one person*, as plainly as that the sun illuminates and warms the earth, we do believe that person has these two natures. The reader will see that the above objection is a mere prevarication.

Another objection is this. "Did a very man come down from heaven? Surely not. Then Christ was not a very man." "I am sure no one will say Abraham's seed came down from heaven."[*] The writer here is either at war with himself, or with inspiration, and we should think with both, for certainly this objection cannot touch Trinitarianism. We do not say that the human body of the Savior came

* Elder O. Barr's " Truth Triumphant," page 33.

down from heaven, but we believe it was he who said, "A body hast thou prepared me," that came down from heaven. In this he seems to be at variance with himself. But when he asserts that Christ was not of the seed of Abraham, he is at war with inspiration. "Concerning his Son Jesus Christ our Lord, which was made of the seed of David, according to the flesh." Rom. 1:3. "Remember that Jesus Christ, of the seed of David, was raised from the dead, according to my Gospel." 2 Tim. 2:8. "He took on him the seed of Abraham." Heb. 2:16. So we see that the writer was not opposing Trinitarianism, but Unitarianism, or the Bible, or both. For the Bible asserts that he was of the seed of Abraham according to the flesh, and that in some sense, he came down from heaven. His humanity *only* died. And while this August Person suffered, nature seemed to be convulsed to its centre, light left the livid sun and fled up to the throne of God. The mountains and valleys shook; the adamantine rocks clave in sunder, as Jesus bowed his majestic head and commended his soul to God his Father.

> "But soon he'll break death's envious chain,
> And in full glory shine,
> O Lamb of God was ever pain,
> Was ever love like thine?"

(8.) He is called the Son of Man—Son of David, and it is said he *sprang from the tribe of Judah.*

He is called a little child (paidion) eight times in the second chapter of the gospel by St. Matthew.

(9.) As he was equal with God in his divine nature, so he makes himself equal with man in his human nature, and consequently declares his inferiority to him. John 14:28. "If you loved me, ye would rejoice because I said I go to my Father; for my Father is greater than I." On the hypothesis that Jesus Christ possessed but *one* nature, it is impossible to reconcile this passage with those where he says, "I and my Father are *one*." "He that hath seen me, hath seen the Father." John 14:9.

Again he says, Rev. 20:10. I am the ROOT and OFFSPRING of David. This declaration is unequivocal. He is, according to his own words, not only the author of the very existence of David, but he is truly his descendant. Now, if he possessed but one nature, as Unitarians so confidently assert, how could this be true? Or, to use the blessed Savior's own words to the Pharisees, who denied that he possessed the nature of God and man, and often accused him of being but a man and yet making himself God:—"If David then called him Lord, how is he his son?" Mat. 22:45. They could not answer him a word. Nor can Unitarians of these days, who affirm that he possesses but one nature, make any better answer than the Pharisees did. So we are brought fairly to the conclusion, that as Christ was David's *offspring* and David's *son*, he possessed his nature; that is, human nature. And, as he was the *Lord* and *Root* of David, he possessed divine nature also. We also conclude, that no solution of these passages can be made, that has any claim to propriety, or merits any degree of re-

gard from intelligent Christians, and careful read-
ers of the sacred volume, in accordance with the
doctrine of any sect of Unitarians on earth.   As
far as our knowledge extends, it is a fundamental
principle with them that Jesus Christ possessed but
one nature.   If, therefore, *that one* nature was " all
divine," how could he be the Son and offspring of
David, according to the flesh?   And if *that one* nature was all *human*, how could he be his *Lord*, and
the *author* of his existence, or, as he styles himself,
" the Root of David?"   But with these remarks concerning the humanity of the *body* of our Savior we shall
leave the candid inquirer after truth to make up his
mind on this point.   We hope this one thought may
revolve in the mind of the reader, that is, The body
of our Savior *must have been human*, or *it was not*,
and if it was not human, it must have been angelic
or divine, and consequently he was not the person
of whom Isaiah spake when he said,   " He was a
MAN of sorrow and acquainted with grief," nor
was the apostle correct who testified, " He was made
like unto his brethren in *all things*," and that the Is-
raelites were the people " whose are the fathers,
and of whom as concerning the *flesh* Christ came,
who is *over* ALL, God blessed forever.   Amen."

II.   Christ possessed a human *soul*.

1. It is as evident, as the Scriptures of divine truth
can make any thing evident, that Jesus Christ *created all things which are in heaven, and on earth,
whether visible, or invisible*, and that without him
was *nothing made* that was made.   The blessed

volume also asserts that Jesus Christ is before *all things*, and by him *all things* consist. Let these passages be kept in view constantly, while we proceed to prove, that he had a human *soul*. This will enable the reader to see whether the proof is sufficient to sustain the proposition.

2. It is a peculiar characteristic of the human soul, or mind, that it constantly *expands* while it is cultivated. Let it also be remembered, that the angels are *created intellectual beings.* Now we are expressly informed, Luke 2:52, That " Jesus increased in *wisdom*," as well as in stature. " *Neura kai osta eisi aloga.*" Nerves and bones are without wisdom, or reason. His *body* could not have increased in wisdom, but it did increase in stature. "The body without the soul is dead." Thus it was with the body of the Lord Jesus, when he said, "Father, into thy hands I commend my spirit." Luke 23:46. Where is the individual who would be guilty of the hardihood to assert that *that intellect* which created the tallest angel that dazzles before the throne of God, should in the space of a few transient days here on earth, be said to "increase in wisdom?" Can it be said that that *mind* which planned the path of *Herschel*, that spread the *belts* across the disk of *Jupiter*, that *set* the mighty *rings* around the planet *Saturn*, that taught the *Comets* their elliptic orbits, increased in wisdom in a few revolving days? Certainly we think no believer in revelation would assert this! Is it not proved by indubitable Scripture testimony,

that JESUS CHRIST created all these planets, and
reared the mighty fabric of the universe? It is so.
Then was that mind that *increased* in *wisdom*, the
identical mind that at the first drafted the plan of
the universe? Most certainly not. Then as candid and rational men we must come to the conclusion that our Lord Jesus possessed a *human mind*,
and that he was in all respects truly man in regard
to his body and mind.

3. It is evident that our Savior possessed a human soul, from the fact that he was *tempted* in all
points like as we are. We are aware that satan
tempts the Christian, by throwing his vile insinua-
tions into the mind. If he possessed no human soul,
and all the soul he had was his divine nature, then
he could not have been tempted, "for God cannot
be tempted with evil, neither tempteth he any man."
In order that he could be our example, and fulfill the
law for us, and in so doing make it honorable, he
must have inherited the capacity of being tempted,
and of course he possessed a human mind, endow-
ed with all the faculties that the mind of our first
parents possessed in their primitive state. There
could have been no propriety in his suffering temptation, as our example, if by his nature, (being des-
titute of a human soul,) he was infinitely above the
power of temptation. Now this must have been
the case, if he had no soul, except the indwelling of
the Godhead, for, as we said before, "God cannot
be tempted."

4. Jesus Christ testified that he had a soul. At

one time he was heard to say, "My soul (psuche) is exceedingly sorrowful." Mark 14:34. Again "my soul (psuche) is troubled, and what shall I say." John 12:27. But perhaps a Unitarian friend may object, "that *this soul* Jesus spake of was not *human*, or like the souls of the rest of mankind, but it was that derived intelligence, whom God authorized and delegated to create the universe, and that it was angelic or *super* angelic." But it should be understood that the angels are spoken of as *spirits*, and not as *souls*. Says an apostle, speaking of angels, "Are not they *all* ministering *spirits*?" (pneumata.) Here they are called spirits. Heb. 1:14, also Heb. 1:7. We frankly acknowledge that the human soul is sometimes termed (pneuma) or the spirit of man. But we have no recollection of angels being described as *souls*, or of their being known by the appellation, PSUCHE.

David, while personating the Savior, says, "Thou wilt not leave my *soul* in *hades*" nor suffer thy holy one, (that is, his body,) to see corruption." Ps. 16:10. Here we have his soul and body brought to view very clearly again. But certainly Christians will not dispute what the Lord Jesus said with his expiring breath. "Father," said he, "into thy hands I commit my spirit." *Gr* "*Pater eis cheiras sou parathesomai to pneuma mou.*" Even with his latest breath, he wishes to commend his soul into the hands of God his Father, thus following the example of many of the illustrious dead who had left the world, saying, "*In manus tuas Domine commendo*
2

spiritum meum." Thus he lived as a man and died as a man, commending his soul to God.

Finally: There is the same evidence that Jesus our Savior possessed a *human body*, that there is that *Peter, John* or *Paul* did; and there is equal evidence that he possessed a *human soul* that there is that he possessed a human body.

CHAPTER II.

*Evidences that the Lord Jesus possessed divine na-
ture, and was in that nature as truly God as he was
man in his human nature.*

UNITARIANS often object to this idea, because they
conclude it is *mysterious.* But we care not whether the idea is said to be mysterious or not mysterious, so we can make our ideas *intelligible.* This is
the mystery an apostle speaks of, when he tells us,
" God was manifest in the flesh, justified in the
spirit, seen of angels, preached unto the Gentiles,
believed on in the world, received up into glory." 1
Tim. 3:16. But will not Unitarians believe any
thing that appears mysterious?

The eternity of God, his *underived* existence, is in
reality mysterious, that is, it is something we cannot comprehend. The view of the universe created and sustained by him is incomprehensible, yet
we generally believe it. We might see a *chain* let
down from a height, and understand that the low-
est link hung on the one above it, and so it might
continue to do to almost an infinite extent, but after all to suppose the highest link in the vast chain,
hung upon and sustained *itself* would seem mysterious. Thus it is with the existence of God. *Gravitation* also is something that people generally suppose has a real existence. We see its effect. The
planetary worlds seem to feel its influence at a great
distance from the centre of the solar system. *Her-*

schel, at the distance of *one thousand eight hundred millions* of miles, obeys its invincible mandate.   A man cannot comprehend himself, nor even a hair that grows from his head. Then certainly it discovers gross folly to undertake to comprehend the incomprehensible Jehovah, and it discovers gross infidelity for a man to say he will believe nothing but what he clearly comprehends.   There are things of which we may have very distinct ideas, which in themselves are utterly *undefinable*. *Gravitation* cannot be *defined*, that is, a man cannot tell what it is, but he may form some idea what it is not. When we say the underived existence of God forms a *proposition*, which in its nature cannot be *defined*, we would not wish to be understood that the proposition itself is one that cannot be made *intelligible*. These remarks we have made, in order to show the inconsistency of Unitarians, in repudiating the doctrine of the *humanity* and *divinity* of our Savior, on the ground that it is mysterious.

1. The existence of Jesus Christ is coetaneous with eternity itself, or with the existence of Jehovah.

David seems to speak of his existence in this sense when he says, " BEFORE the mountains were brought forth, or even *thou hadst formed* the *earth* and the world, even *from* EVERLASTING *to* EVERLASTING thou art GOD." Ps. 90:2. He thought the Creator existed from eternity to eternity, as far as thought can extend backward, nay, farther, or farther than it can reach into futurity.

This is the highest and clearest description of the
eternity of God to which words in human language
can possibly reach. But it undoubtedly will be objected by Unitarians, that " this language does not
refer to Jesus Christ at all." Well, it does refer to
the Creator who formed the earth and the world,
and it only remains to prove who was the Creator,
in order to settle this question. It must, we think,
be admitted, that the Creator was from eternity to
eternity, according to the words of the text. Then
we have found one being that has eternally existed.
But a question of some importance on this point is,
Who was the Creator? We answer, *God* was the
Creator of all things. This we trust we shall be
able to prove. We find that the Almighty has said,
" I am the Lord that maketh all things, that stretcheth forth the heavens *alone*, that spreadeth abroad
the earth *by myself*." Isa. 44:24. Again. " For
thus saith the Lord, that created the heavens, God
himself that formed the earth and made it; I am
the Lord, and there is none else." Isa. 45:18. It is
certainly clear that he who formed the earth possessed *underived existence*, because he is said to be
" from everlasting to everlasting." This perhaps
a Unitarian would admit. But we ask again, Who
was the Creator? We answer again: It was that
person in the *trinity* whom we call *Jesus Christ*.
This we also can readily prove. " For by him were
all things created, that are in the heaven, and that
are in earth, *visible* and *invisible*, whether they
be thrones, or dominions, or principalities, or pow-

ers: all things were created by him, and for him: and
he is before all things, and by him all things consist."
Col. 1:16, 17. "And thou, Lord, in the beginning
hast laid the foundation of the earth, and the heavens are the works of thy hands." Heb. 1:10. "All
things were made by him, and without him was not
any thing made that was made." John 1:3. These
last three texts are all spoken in reference to the
Lord Jesus, as the reader may see by consulting his
Bible. If, then, we have succeeded in proving that
the Creator of all things had an existence from eternity to eternity, we have proved also that Jesus
Christ has the same underived existence in respect
to his divine nature, and consequently our *first* proposition is sustained. But it is objected, "that Jesus
Christ is not in any sense self-existent, because he
made the world, and so on, by delegated power."
Now this objection defeats itself, from these considerations.

(1.) Creative power is an inherent attribute of
the self-existent and eternal God, and he cannot
delegate his attributes.

(2.) If Jesus Christ did it for him, and he was not
truly God himself, then it follows that Jesus Christ
created *himself*, "for he created *all things* that are
created," and there can be but one uncreated being
in the universe.

(3.) It contradicts the Bible, for that (as we have
shown from Isaiah) proves that the *Creator* did it
by himself ALONE. If Jesus Christ created these
things, and he was not truly God, then Jehovah did

it not, as he says he did. Hear him again, "I am
the LORD that maketh all things, that stretcheth
forth the heavens *alone*, that spreadeth abroad the
earth BY MYSELF." If the works of creation
and the language which the inspired writers use in
respect to Christ, do not prove his self-existence, we
can certainly have no proof of any self-existent being in the universe. We have now proved that *Jehovah* created all things, and the *Lord Jesus* created
all things, and it follows that they are *one* in nature,
that is, that Jesus Christ in his divine nature is God,
or there are *two* Almighty, Self-existent Creators!
which is an absurdity.

2. *God by the mouth of the prophet* speaks of the
Messiah as possessing *uncreated existence.* "But
thou Bethlehem Ephrata, though thou be little
among the thousands of Judah, yet out of thee shall
he come forth unto me, that is to be Ruler in Israel,
whose goings forth have been from of *old ;* even from
EVERLASTING." Mich. 5:2. This corresponds
precisely with what the Lord Jesus says of himself
" I am the *first* and the *last.* I am he that liveth
and was dead, and behold I am alive forevermore,
Amen; and have the keys of death and hell." Rev.
1:17, 18. "I am Alpha and Omega, the beginning and
the ending, saith the Lord, which is, and which was,
and which is to come, the ALMIGHTY. Rev. 1:8.
Here is testimony that Jesus Christ is (in some sense
at least,) the FIRST and the LAST; that is, he is
the fountain of all created existence, and in him is
the final consummation of time and things. Jeho-

vah applies to himself the titles of "*first* and *last*,"
and says beside him " there is no God." Isa. 44:6.
If, then, the terms first and last, when applied to Jehovah, prove his *uncreated existence* and eternity,
what do the same terms prove when Jesus Christ
applies them to himself—and teaches us that He is
the First and the Last?   God also testifies, as we
have just seen, that Christ is one " whose goings
forth have been from of *old*, even from *everlasting*."
Now, shall we believe that his " goings forth have
been from *everlasting*," from the countless dates of
eternity, or shall we not? It is either as God has said,
or it is *not so*.   How then must it appear, to see a
man, a *finite* man, rise up and say, " Jesus Christ is
not unoriginated," that is, " he is not from eternity
in his existence?" But, alas! how this sounds when
it comes from a Christian, and a *professed minister*
of Jesus Christ!!   Is it possible that *believers* in the
truths of revelation shall use the same language in
relation to the character of Christ that infidels
do? and *both agree* that there was never any incarnation of the Divine Being?   From the foregoing
remarks and quotations from the holy book of God,
it is evidently proved that Jesus Christ in his divine nature is *uncreated*, and if uncreated his existence is *eternal*, and if his existence is *eternal* he is
God.   Then to his name be ascribed Glory, Power
and Dominion forever and ever.

CHAPTER III.

A brief view of the worship which is addressed to our Lord Jesus Christ, and which acknowledges him to be God.

> " THOU whose all providential eye surveys,
> Whose hand directs, whose Spirit fills and warms
> Creation, and holds empire far beyond !
> Eternity's Inhabitant august !
> Of *two* eternities amazing Lord !
> One, past ere man's or angels had began!
> Aid, while I rescue from the foe's assault"
> The holy worship of thine only Son,
> Who from Eternity was God with thee !
> Aid thou my pen while I shall now describe,
> " A theme forever, and for all, of weight,
> Of moment infinite ! but relished most,
> By those who love thee most, who most adore."

If the Bible proves that Jesus Christ is worshiped on earth and in heaven as God, certainly this must end all dispute as it relates to the Godhead of the adorable Savior. We are expressly forbidden by the Almighty Jehovah, to fall down and worship *any thing* in heaven or in earth, or in the waters under the earth, save *himself alone.* This idea is as clearly set forth on the pages of inspiration, as it is that there is any God at all. And it is as clearly shown by the same book that Jesus Christ is worshiped as God, as it is that Jehovah is thus worshiped. The man who reads the volume of divine truth and does not see this must shut his eyes:—

> . . . . "And bold with joy,
> Forth from his dark and lonely hiding place.

3

Portentous sight! Owlet infidelity!
Sailing on obscene wings athwart the noon,
Drops his blue-fringed lids, and holds them close,
And hooting at the glorious sun in heaven,
Cries out, "*Where is it?*"

1. Jesus Christ is worshiped jointly with the
Father and the Holy Spirit by his people both in
heaven and on earth. In proof of this we will consider the numerous benedictions of an apostle on
the Christian churches. "Grace to you and peace
from God our Father and the Lord Jesus Christ."
Rom. 1:7. 1 Cor. 1:3. 2 Cor. 1:2. Gal. 1:3. Eph. 1:2,
and 6:23. Phil. 3. Col. 1:2. 1 Thess. 1:1. 2 Thess.
1:2. Here the same blessing from God the Father
and the Lord Jesus Christ is conferred by an inspired
man no less than *eleven* times. The Father and
Son are associated together without any disparity
in their characters, or claims to supreme divine
worship! "Go ye therefore and teach all nations,
baptizing them in (eis) the name of the Father, and
of the Son nd of the Holy Ghost. Mat. 28:18.
It is admitted on all hands that baptism is an act of
religious worship, and taking the common English
version as it stands we have it "In the name," that
is, by *the authority* of the sacred three. But as Unitarians believe the Holy Ghost to be only "an *energy, influence,* or *power,* of The Father, it follows, if
they are correct, that baptism is performed by the
authority of *Jehovah* and a *created being* and an
influence! This would be mere tautology. When
the person is baptized in the name of the *Father,*

certainly that includes all his *attributes*, then why baptize in the name of one of these attributes again? But who will deny that Jesus Christ is worshiped in this act even as the Father is worshiped?

Every person who reads the original of this passage, knows that the literal translation is, " Go ye, therefore, teach all nations, baptizing them *into* (eis) the name," &c. *Eis to onoma* literally means, as we have stated already, *into the name*. With this translation of the preposition *eis* Unitarianism necessarily sinks one step lower. The candidate is baptized into the recognition of the Father, Son, and Holy Ghost as his God. A late writer on Unitarianism* has tried to free his system from the burden this passage throws upon it; but every scholar who reads his work will see that he tried in vain. But Christ has settled this point when he says, that " All men should honor the Son, even as they honor the Father." John 5:23. If the Father be honored as Creator, then the Son is to be honored in the same manner. If the Father be honored as *Almighty*, *Preserver*, or as the God of boundless perfections and glory; the Son claims the same honor. Again, we read " Grace, mercy, and peace, from God the Father and from our Lord Jesus Christ." 1 Tim. 1:2. Tit. 1:4. 2 John 3. Rev. 1:4, 5. " Every tongue shall confess that Jesus Christ is Lord to the glory of God the Father." Phil. 2:11. " Our Lord Jesus Christ, and God, even our Father, com-

* Mr. Morgridge, a preacher of the Christian denomination.

fort your hearts and stablish you." 2 Thess. 6:16.
"Every creature which is in heaven and in earth,
heard I saying, Blessing and Honor and Glory and
Power be unto him that sitteth upon the throne and
unto the Lamb forever and ever." Rev. 5:13. From
the above declaration of the word of God, it is evident that the *worship* done to the Father is also
proffered to the Son, that it is the same in quality
and essence. Not the least shade of a difference
can be made to appear. Then we have fully sustained the proposition that Jesus Christ is worshiped jointly with the Father and Holy Spirit, both
in heaven and on earth. Nor does it seem rational
that the Father would be associated with a *mere
creature* in such acts of solemn worship, after having expressly said that he *alone* would be worshiped and adored by all the saints on earth and all the
spirits that shine in his presence above.

2. Acts of divine worship offered to Jesus Christ
alone both in heaven and on earth.

> " All hail the great Immanuel's name,
>   Let angels prostrate fall,
> Bring forth the royal diadem,
>   And crown *Him* LORD of *All.*

Dear to the saints of God is the privilege of worshiping him who washed them in his own blood
and made them Kings and Priests to God. Though
they may be accused by Unitarians of "worshiping
God and *two* other *beings*," or of being gross idolaters, yet while they think of the bower of prayer,

they say, with bosoms heaving with love to the Redeemer, and to the Lord Jesus:

> " How oft have I knelt on the evergreen there,
>   And pour̥d out my soul *to my Savior in prayer*."

Says the blessed Savior, " Where two or three
are met in my name, there am I." Mat. 18:20.   To
meet in his name, is to meet for his worship. " And
they stoned Stephen, calling upon God and saying,
Lord Jesus, receive my spirit." Acts 7:59.   The
word " God" is not in the original, we frankly allow.   And it is strange that Unitarians should seize
this circumstance, thinking that leaving the word
God out, would benefit their system.   Who did Stephen pray to with his dying breath, when he said,
Lord Jesus, receive my spirit?   The word (epika-
loumenon,) which is translated " calling upon, and
saying," literally means *to invoke*, or *to pray*, therefore it is evident he prayed to the Lord Jesus.   Who
else would the saint of God commit his soul to,   at
this last crisis?   But this prayer of Stephen, the
Martyr, A. D. 33, was not a singular prayer.   The
primitive Christians, in the days of the apostles,
prayed to Jesus Christ usually.   Says Paul, " Unto
the church of God that is at Corinth, to them that
are sanctified in Christ Jesus, called to be saints, with
all that in every place *call upon the name of Jesus
Christ our Lord*, both theirs and ours." 1 Cor. 1:
2.   No rational man can help seeing, that according
to these words, *all the saints* called upon the name
of Jesus Christ, that is, they prayed to him.   Did
they pray to a mere *creature?*   How appalling the

thought. They were bred from infancy to worship
God *only*, and they had the most convincing proof
of the Godhead of the Savior, or they would not
have worshiped him as God. But we have a number of passages more to this very point. "In the
name of Jesus Christ of Nazareth, rise up and
walk." Acts. 3:6. This is a most solemn appeal to
his Almighty power. "Wash away thy sins, calling
on the name of the Lord." Acts 22:16. "The
Lord Jesus Christ be with thy spirit." 2 Tim. 4:
22. "But grow in grace, and in the knowledge of
our Lord and Savior Jesus Christ, to whom be glory, now and forever. Amen." 2 Pet. 3:18. "When
he bringeth his first begotten into the world, he saith,
Let all the angels of God worship him." Heb. 1:6.
"And I beheld and heard the voice of many angels round about the throne, and the beasts, and the
elders, and the number of them was ten thousand
times ten thousand, and thousands of thousands,
saying with a loud voice, Worthy is the Lamb that
was slain to receive Power, and Riches, and Wisdom, and Strength, and Honor, and Glory, and
Blessing." Rev. 5:11, 12. Are not the loftiest
strains of angelic worship due to the Lamb even in
heaven?'and shall we be called idolaters because
we worship him in feebler strains below?

> "We'll crowd his gates with thankful songs,
>   High as the heavens our voices raise,
> And earth, with her ten thousand tongues,
>   Shall fill his courts with sounding praise."

Thus we see the Savior is worshiped in heaven,

and on earth alone, and as God. But one or two testimonies more in regard to the devotions of the apostles and early disciples of Christ. "And they prayed and said, Thou, Lord, that knowest the hearts of all men." Acts 1:24. The church was his peculiar care, for Jesus Christ was the head over all things to the church, and it was with the utmost propriety, that they should call upon him while they were choosing a person to fill the same place and office, that one whom he had formerly chosen himself, had occupied. It is also evident that the disciples, after his resurrection, applied the titles *Lord* and *God* to him indifferently. "Lord, wilt thou at this time restore again the kingdom to Israel." Acts 1:6. "Philip, speaking to him says, My Lord and my God." John 20:28.

· But lastly on this point. We read in the beginning of the ninth chapter of the Acts, that Saul breathed out threatenings and slaughter against the disciples of the Lord. When the Lord appeared to him, he inquires, "Who art thou, Lord," "and the Lord said, I am Jesus." The same Lord appeared to Ananias, and Ananias said to him, "Lord, I have heard by many of this man, how much evil he hath done to *thy saints* at Jerusalem, and here he hath authority from the chief priests to bind ALL THAT CALL UPON THY NAME." Ananias went to Saul and told him, "The Lord even Jesus that appeared unto thee in the way as thou comest, hath SENT ME, that thou mightest receive thy sight." This same Lord told Ananias that Saul

was a chosen vessel unto him, and that he must
suffer much for his name's sake. Acts 9:16. But
when Paul rehearsed this story in his defence.
Acts 22, he says, " Ananias came unto me, and stood,
and said unto me, Brother Saul, receive thy sight,
and the same hour I looked up upon him. And he
said *the* GOD *of our fathers* hath chosen thee,"
&c. From this we see that the Christians of the
apostles' days *prayed* or *called upon the name* of the
Lord Jesus generally, and this was a distinguishing
characteristic of Christians, that they prayed to Jesus Christ. Again, we see that the same person is
called *Jesus*, *Lord*, and *God*, in this transaction,
even the God of the Hebrew Fathers. Certainly
this is sufficient evidence that Jesus Christ was, and
is, worshiped on earth, and in heaven as God, and
consequently, when Trinitarians worship Him as
such, they cannot justly be termed idolaters.

CHAPTER IV.

The Omniscience of our Lord Jesus Christ.

THAT our Savior is omniscient is flatly contradicted by Unitarians. But if we prove he had this *attribute* of Jehovah, (and it is presumed that no one will pretend that God ever delegated his attributes,) that it belonged to our Savior, that he possessed it, we shall prove Unitarianism to be false in another fundamental point. Omniscience is that attribute of God, by which he knows *the thoughts*, and even the *imaginations* of the thoughts of all hearts. He sees the end from the beginning, and truly knows all the intermediate circumstances. Now, if we can prove that this power was possessed by our Lord, we shall prove him, in his divine nature, to be God, or we must acknowledge that there are two beings possessing this attribute, which can be possessed by Jehovah alone; this again would be an absurdity. But we will bring forward the testimony of our Lord himself on this point. "As the Father knoweth me, even so know I the Father." John 10:15. If this asserts the omniscience of the Father, which none, we think, will deny; it also proves the omniscience of the Son. What *man* would dare face his Maker with a blasphemy like this, and say, "I know all about him who made me, as well as he knows me?" What angel would dare lift up his head before the throne, and say, "I know Him that sits on that throne as he knows me?" Angels

would tremble to hear such blasphemy avowed by
any created being! Indeed, it would be the height
of blasphemy, for any created being, in heaven, or
on earth, or in hell, to make such a statement as this!
This testimony of Jesus Christ must make the
council of anti-christ tremble. Remember that the
Son states, that he knows the Father, *in the same
sense* that the Father knows him. This includes
the heighths and depths of omniscience! Even the
mind of God was known by him; his *plans*, his *designs*, were all known; the stupendous scheme of
salvation was concerted by the *Father, Son*, and
Holy Ghost, before all worlds. But mark their
love for man.

> ———————— "Eternal love—
> Harp lift up thy voice on high—Eternal Love—
> Eternal sovereign love and sovereign grace,
> . Wisdom, and power, and mercy infinite !
> The Father, Son, and Holy Spirit, God,
> Devised the wondrous plan—devised, achieved;
> And in achieving, made the marvel more."

But to the testimony again. "Jesus knowing
their thoughts." Mat. 12:25. "He knew what was
in man, and needed not that *any should testify of
man*." John 2:24. "Therefore, judge nothing
before the time, until the Lord come, who both will
bring to light the hidden things of darkness, and
will make manifest the *counsels of the hearts*, and
then shall every man have praise of God." 1 Cor.
4:5. "Thou, Lord, which knowest the hearts of all
men, show whether of these two thou hast chosen."

Acts 1:24. "Lord, (said Peter,) thou knowest *all things, thou knowest* that I love thee." John 21: 17. "I am he that searcheth the reins and the heart." Rev. 2:23. We might multiply scripture testimony on this subject; but in the mouth of two or three witnesses, the truth will be established. If these texts do not prove that our Lord Jesus was omniscient, there can be no proof brought from the sacred volume to sustain the idea that Jehovah is omniscient. We have then the same testimony of the omniscience of Christ that we have of his *existence;* for we have proved it by his own testimony and the testimony of his apostles. If we repose confidence in their testimony of the existence of such a person as Christ, why not place the same confidence in their testimony concerning his character. He so perfectly understood all the secret windings of the human soul, that he *needed* not that *any* should instruct him. Infidels generally acknowledge the existence of such a person as Jesus Christ; but his character they doubt. There is, in fact, no person that *knows* that there is no God, yet many doubt it. Neither is there any one that knows that Jesus Christ was not omniscient, yet some doubt it. This is all they can do, unless they are possessed with the attribute of omniscience themselves. Very many may be found, who have commenced doubting one truth of revelation after another, because it could not be completely comprehended by their feeble minds, until they have landed themselves on the dangerous shores of infidelity. The very mo-

ment that *one* truth which is plainly taught in the
Bible, is rejected, the way to infidelity is paved.
To that individual

> " The gate of hell stands open night and day,
>   Smooth the descent, and easy is the way !"

It seems to us to be marvellous credulity, for a
man to believe that a *creature*, a finite being, created at first and still sustains the universe. And it
is equally marvellous incredulity, to disbelieve in
the omniscience of the Creator and Governor of the
universe. A man that can believe that a *creature*
made all things—all intelligences, in heaven and
in earth—and yet that that creature did not possess
the power of knowing all things of himself; that
is, inherently, need never charge his fellow men
with believing "mysteries," while his own theory
contains the mystery, that a *creature created himself!!*

There is but *one* uncreated being ; and Jesus
Christ created all created beings: therefore, if he
is a created being, he must have created himself;
and if he is uncreated, he must be that *one* uncreated being, and consequently God. Now this proposition can be, and is, as clearly demonstrated, as
that "two straight lines cannot enclose a space."
Indeed, it is an *axiom*, and needs no demonstra-
tion; for it is self-evident the moment it is mentioned. To say that a *creature* was *uncreated* is folly.
And to say that an *uncreated being* is a creature, is
consummate folly. Now Jesus Christ is either a
creature *wholly*, or in *part*, or he *is not*. If he is

uncreated in *part*, he is so far God. If he is a
creature entire, he was self-created entire, or he did
not MAKE *all things*, as the Bible expressly declares;
and this last ground makes us *infidels.* And is it
the case that the Almighty *Creator* was not omniscient? If he was not, there is no being that *is;* and
consequently there is no God—no all-wise God, in
the universe! No such God as the Bible describes,
and the fool had it right, when he said in his heart:
" There is no God." If there is no such God as
the Bible describes, it is probable there is none at
all. While we follow out the logical result of the
doctrine that makes the Creator himself a *creature,*
how it chills the flames of devotion and piety; and
how soul-abhorrent it is to the devoted follower of
the Lord Jesus Christ, who is over all, God blessed
forever. Amen.

But to impress this thought on the mind of the
reader, we will give it the form of a syllogism.

Jesus Christ created every creature in the universe.

Jesus Christ himself was a creature.

Therefore, Jesus Christ created himself.

There is no such thing as evading this, and this,
with all its absurdity, is Unitarianism—naked, plain,
unvarnished Unitarianism. But we will try the
propositions of Trinitarians, by the same sollogis-
tic method of reasoning.

That being that is self-existent is God.

Jesus Christ is self-existent.

Ergo: Jesus Christ is God.

The Lord Jesus Christ is either created or he is not; and here is the unequivocal, logical result of both propositions. Which do you choose?

If the Lord Jesus is a *finite* being, if he is not *omniscient*, paradventure while his children pray, his mind is occupied with some other business, and he will not know that they are calling upon him, and especially if he is finite, and *occupies but one place at the same time*, he is not able to meet with all that meet in his name, and for his worship, and consequently cannot fulfill his precious promise. In this case, it would be totally unsafe to commit the keeping of our departing spirits into his hands, as did the holy Stephen. But with his own declarations before us, we will run all the risk there is in believing in his omnipresence, and omniscience.

CHAPTER V.

The wisdom of our Lord Jesus Christ, is the wisdom of Jehovah: therefore, in this respect, he is God.

CHRIST truly possessed all the deep treasures of uncreated *wisdom*, even the *wisdom of Jehovah*, and this again, thus far, constitutes his perfect divinity. We wish it still borne in mind that Christ had, as we have clearly proved by God's holy word, the nature that other men have, that is, *human nature.* This point, we conclude, has been fully sustained. And as it respects his divine nature, we have already proved, that the *existence* of Christ *was underived*, that he is *worshiped as God*, in heaven and on earth, and that he was possessed of the *attribute* of *omniscience* in its full extent. The object of the present chapter is to show that his wisdom was not the wisdom of a *created mind*, but it was that wisdom which flows alone from the unfailing fountain of his Godhead, and is boundless as the realm of infinite extent over which the Almighty sways his sceptre. In proof, then, of the present position, we appeal to the veracity of the holy volume, which says, "To the *only wise God* our Savior, be *glory*, and *majesty*, dominion and power, both now and ever. Amen." Jude, 25. Here Jesus Christ is addressed as the *only wise* GOD OUR SAVIOR, and the highest tribute of

praise ascribed to his venerable name. Again, he
is said to be "*Christ*, the power of *God, and* the
wisdom of God." 1 Cor. 1:24.   And an apostle
informs us that " in him are hid *all the treasures* of
wisdom and knowledge." Mark: ALL *the* TREAS-
URES of wisdom and knowledge are hid in him.
Is there any wisdom which he has not? Here, then,
he is plainly described as possessing infinite and
unbounded wisdom, which can belong only to that
Being whom we call *God*.   His boundless wisdom
is most clearly seen in the works of his hands.
For,

> " Who turns his eye on nature's midnight face,
> But must inquire—' What hand behind the scene,
> What arm Almighty put these wheeling globes
> In motion, and wound up the vast machine ?
> Who rounded in his hand, these spacious orbs ?
> Who rolled them flaming through the dark profound,
> Numerous as the glittering gems of morning dew,
> Or sparks, from populous cities in a blaze,
> And set the bosom of old night on fire ?
> Peopled the deserts, and made horror smile ?' "

If, then, his works do not prove his uncreated wisdom and design, we can have no idea that any
being in the universe possesses these qualifica-
tions.

St. Paul unhesitatingly affirms that "in him
dwelleth all the fullness of the *Godhead* bodily."
(*Theotetos somatikos*) Col. 2:9.   He does not say,
" the God" dwelleth in him, but the *Godhead* (*theotetos*.)   This original word signifies " *State of being, or divine nature*, the infinite attributes essen-

tial to such a nature." Bodily, (somatikos,) signifies *truly*, or *really*, in opposition to a *typical*, or
figurative residence. Then we understand that
God dwelt in the person of Jesus Christ *essentially*, substantially, and *personally*, as the human soul
dwells in, and vivifies the body. This explains
what he said to Philip. "He that hath seen me,
hath seen the Father;" and "I am in the Father,
and the Father in me." Then, if the Bible can be
relied upon as testimony, we think this point, also,
sustained. If the Bible is not to be taken as deci-
sive evidence, we must change our position, and,
instead of proving the holy doctrine of the divinity
of Jesus Christ from that, we must turn and strike
against gross infidelity and prove the Bible to be
the truth of God. But admitting the blessed Bible
to be true, as we trust all who profess the Christian religion will do, we may safely proceed to
show the contaminating error of denying the divinity and humanity of the Son of God. Were it not
for this blessed mirror, that reflects upon us the
purity of the upper world, we should know but little of the mode of the supreme existence. Without this lamp to illumine our benighted world, we
might wander as fugitives, in darkness, through the
scenes of this transient world, and sink at last, in
tempests and in storms, beneath the sable waves of
an eternal night, when none should weep our fall,
and none record our name. But, thanks be to Heav-
en, for the inexpressible gift of the holy volume.
4

Then why not believe its most positive declarations?

If Jesus Christ is the *wisdom* and *power* of God, he is so *inherently*, or this wisdom and power is delegated to him. Shall we suppose that God delegated his own *wisdom* and power? Candor will reply no; and yet we may as well expect that he delegated all his *wisdom*, as that he delegated *creative power*. But see what had God left to himself after delegating his power and wisdom? If Jesus Christ was not God, as Unitarians assert, but only " a god" in the subordinate sense that Moses was called god, then the result is, that the Father was *inactive* or inert, while Christ has been *creating* the worlds, and that the Father had neither wisdom nor power, because Christ had all wisdom, and all power, in heaven and in earth! Now the fact is that Jesus Christ, the *wisdom* and power of God, was one with God from eternity, as says the word of inspiration. " I was set up from everlasting, from the beginning or ever the earth was. When there were no depths I was brought forth, when there were no fountains abounding with water. Before the mountains were settled, before the hills was I brought forth. When he prepared the heavens, l was there; when he set a compass upon the face of the deep, when he established the clouds above, when he strengthened the fountains of the deep; when he gave to the sea his decree, that the water should not pass his commandment, when he appointed the foundations of the earth: then I was by him, as one brought up with him, and I was daily his delight, rejoicing always before him." Prov. 8:23—30.

CHAPTER VI.

The Omnipresence of our Lord Jesus Christ.

THERE are, we think, very few who profess to believe the record God has given of his Son, who would *avow* the doctrine that the Almighty was confined to any particular location.   Very few Christians would fall in with the idea that Jehovah could be in only one place at a time.   There is but *one* omnipresent being of which we can possibly form any conception whatever.   That being that can be present in all parts of the world and in the celestial regions at the same time, must be omnipresent.   If that being is not omnipresent, we have no proof of any omnipresent being.   But that there is such a being, no believer in God will deny, or seriously doubt.   If, then, we can prove that Jesus Christ is omnipresent, that is, that he can be in more places than one at the same time, we shall prove him to be God, in his divine nature.   We will appeal to his own words on this point.   "Where *two* or *three* are gathered together in my name, there am I in the midst of them."   Mat. 18:20.   "Lo I am with you *always*, even to the end of the world."   Mat. 28: 20.   "And no man hath ascended up to heaven, but he that came down from heaven, even the Son of man, which is in heaven."   John 3:13.

1. Wherever his children meet for worship, there says the Savior, AM I. While his saints are assembled, they do not have to wait for him to come, but

he is already there. Ten thousand congregations
meet on every holy Sabbath in his name, and *a*
find his promise verified. The old, grey-headed
veteran of the cross, while in the sanctuary of God,
feels his heart warmed with the presence of his Savior, and with his countenance brightening up with
rapture, exclaims, "I know my Redeemer lives, I
feel him in my soul, the hope of glory." Says the
young convert, while tears gather in his eyes, "I
know in whom I have believed; I feel he is with
me now." If, indeed, the blessed Jesus was not
omnipresent, what a death-blow would it strike at
the root of Christian enjoyment. The Christian
says from the centre of his soul:

> "Blest Jesus, what delicious fare,
> How sweet thine entertainments are,
> Never did angels taste above,
> Redeeming grace and dying love."

Take Jesus out of the assembly, and all is gone;
and while he is present, if a prison, or a pit, is the
home of the Christian, he feels that he has the best
of company. The martyr has found him to be
present to help him in the curling flames, while the
hosts of heaven meekly bow before him and cast
their crowns at his feet. Christian reader, do you
not feel and know him to be with you while you
meet for his worship? Would not the chill of
death freeze your devotions, if you thought that Jesus was not present with all his children? and with
you?

2. Wherever his people may be, his promise can cheer them. "Lo I am with you." While the missionary is crossing the trackless deep, Jesus is with him, and at the same time he feels that he is with his brethren and sisters whom he has left, and upon whose faces he has gazed for the last time until he meets them " where no farewell tear is shed." The minister of Jesus, while he faces the storms of opposition and of hell, confides in his omnipresent Savior. If this were not so, how sad must be his soul, while called to leave his father, mother, brothers, and sisters, and no Jesus to go with him. How this idea must paralyze his zeal for God. But to know he has his Jesus within, reigning in his soul, and fighting his battles for him, nerves his heart with holy ardor for the arduous task. Every Christian in the dying hour, wants a present Savior, and may have *one*, even him who died and lives forever more.

> " All hail! triumphant Lord,
>   Eternal be thy reign ;
> Behold the nations wait,
>   To wear thy gentle chain.
> When earth and time are known no more,"
> Thy throne shall stand forever sure."

3. What he said to Nicodemus proves beyond the shade of a doubt that he was omnipresent. While he is now speaking to him, and conversing with him, he says he is even *in heaven*. No one will pretend that he was trying to deceive Nicodemus, yet if he was not omnipresent, he was practicing a most infamous deception upon him. He

declared the ubiquity of his nature in positive terms. Who, we would ask, but "he who fills heaven and earth," could, in truth, make such a declaration as our Savior here made? Now the question is, shall we believe what Jesus Christ said, or shall we not? If we do credit his assertion, can we believe him to be a mere creature? After all he has said on this subject, Unitarians maintain that he is not an omnipresent being, but a finite creature, and the Holy Spirit only an *energy*, *attribute*, or *power* of Jehovah. Let the candid reader now say, if we have not proved the omnipresence of the Lord Jesus Christ? According to his own words, can he not be present on earth and in heaven at the same time? Truth will answer he can. If he is omnipresent, Unitarianism is found to be erroneous in a most fundamental point. We have on no point yet exhausted the Bible testimonies, nor do we wish to, for it would be quoting almost the entire Bible. The doctrine of the *divinity* of Christ, and of the *trinity* in *unity* of the Godhead, runs through the whole blessed volume. If two or three positive declarations of God's word, will not prove a proposition, which is in accordance with the general tenor of the Bible, to be the truth, we must despair of proving any thing by the Bible.

CHAPTER VII.

The Immutability of our Lord Jesus Christ.

NOTWITHSTANDING all that may have been said
by Unitarians in opposition to the doctrine of the *immutability* of Jesus Christ, yet we think this hypothesis is easily sustained by the word of inspiration. Men are subject to changes, as says one of
old, " Thou changest his countenance and sendest
him away." Angels are likewise changeable, and
are charged with folly. But there is one being who
changes not, and "with whom is no variableness
nor shadow of turning." James 1:17. It must be
evident to any candid mind that that Being who
eternally was and is the same must be uncreated.
Then, if we prove Jesus Christ to have been in any
sense *immutable*, thus far we shall prove him to be
God. We will therefore hear the words of the Almighty himself as testimony on this controverted
point. " And of the angels he saith, who maketh his
angels spirits and his ministers a flame of fire, but
unto the Son he saith, " Thy throne, O GOD, is
forever and ever, a sceptre of righteousness is the
sceptre of thy kingdom." Heb. 1:7, 8. Here we
have the word of Jehovah to prove his throne of
power to be (*aiona tou aionos,*) eternal, and eternally the same. " Jesus Christ *the same*, yesterday,
to-day *and forever*," (aionos.) Heb. 13:8. Here
then is a sure foundation for the saints of God to
build their hopes of eternal felicity upon. The

things of this life are fluctuating, but the Creator, and Redeemer, and the Savior of the world changes not.   He is the same.   The terms "yesterday, to-day, and forever," fully express his eternity.   The same language is applied to Jehovah; and the same sense is conveyed when God said to Moses, " I am that I AM." Exod. 3:14.   Now this august title is often applied to Jesus Christ, to denote his eternal existence; that is, eternity of duration is said to belong to him.   Then, if the Bible proves the immutability of Jehovah, it does also that of our Lord Jesus Christ.   For he spread out the mighty curtain of the skies, and yet

> " His throne eternal ages stood,
>   Ere seas or hills were made;
>   He is the ever-living God,
>   Were all the nations dead."

How exceedingly vain would it be to apply to any *creature* in the universe the titles applied to Jesus Christ.   To which of the *angels* could Jehovah say, " *Thy throne*, O GOD, *is forever* and ever?" He could say this to none of the angels, because they are *creatures*; that is, they are created beings. The Son is either a creature or he is *not*, and

If he is *uncreated*, he is self-existent;

If he is *self existent*, he is eternal;

And if he is *eternal*, he must be God;

Therefore, if Jesus Christ is *uncreated*, he must be God.

Then, upon his Almighty, *immutable* arm we may
5

rest secure; but if he is not immutable, he may fail
us in the time of our greatest need. "And if the
foundation be destroyed, what shall the righteous
do?" But, notwithstanding all the attacks that
have been made upon his precious character, by
hell, anti-christ, and the devil, he still is to the
Christian his only *refuge*, his *hiding-place*, and his
everlasting reward beyond the grave. His language is, while he reflects on him who bore his sorrows on the tree, "Jesus is all to my soul."
Yet

> "Some take him a *creature* to be,
>   A man or an angel at most:
> Sure these have not feelings like me,
>   Nor know themselves wretched and lost.
> So guilty, so helpless am I,
>   I could not confide in his word,
> Nor on his protection rely,
>   Unless I could call him MY LORD.
>
> If asked what of Jesus I think,
>   Though still my best thoughts are but poor,
> I say he 's my meat and my drink,
>   My life, and my strength, and my store;
> My shepherd, my husband, my friend,
>   My Savior from sin and from thrall;
> My hope from beginning to end,
>   My portion, my LORD, and my *all*."

It is evident that Jesus Christ could not have been
immutable, and the same from eternity to eternity,
if he was ever created. The *Word*, or Wisdom,
(Logos,) that John speaks of as being in the beginning with God, and as being God, must have been a
substance or an *attribute*. If in his pre-existent

state, he was an *attribute* of Jehovah, and was a created being as Unitarians would have him, then it follows, unavoidably, that God created his *attributes!* And if he is a *substance* created by the Father, how could he be God? "In the beginning was the Word, and the Word was with God, and the Word was God." John 1:1. If the *first* time in this text, John uses the word God (Theos,) to signify *Jehovah*, what does it mean in the *second* use he makes of it? " *The Word was God.*" Is it possible that there is an infinite difference in the sense of this very word, used as it is, *twice* in the same sentence? There is an infinite difference between God and *any* of his creatures. So we come to the conclusion, irresistibly, that as Jehovah is *immutable* or unchangeable, so is the Son also in his divine nature.

CHAPTER VIII.

The Omnipotence of our Lord Jesus Christ.

FEW, we think, in the Christian world would aver
that almighty, unlimited power, could be possessed by
any being in the universe, but God alone. If there
can be *more than one* omnipotent being, there can
be more than one self-existent and eternal being.
But the Scriptures assure us that there is only *One*
living and true God. Then, again, if we prove Jesus
Christ to have possessed omnipotent power, or that
he is almighty, we shall, by so doing, show clearly
the fallacy of that doctrine which makes him a creature. It is denied by Unitarians that Jesus Christ
is ever called Almighty in the Bible. We will see.
But, in the first place, we wish to remark, *that no
creature is omnipotent.* In Isa. 9:6, we read that
" he shall be called *the mighty .GOD*," and not *a*
mighty god! " I am alpha and omega, the beginning and the ending, saith the Lord, which is, and
which was, and which is to come, the ALMIGH-
TY. Rev. 1:8. Again, "Thus saith the Lord, the
king of Israel and his redeemer, the Lord of hosts.
I am the first and *I am the last*, and beside me there
is no God." Isa. 44:6. "These things saith the
first, and the last, (which was dead and is alive.")
Rev. 2:8. The terms *first* and *last* signify one
whose existence never began and will never cease.
No angel can, in truth, say, that he is the *first cause,*
and in himself is the consummation of all things.

No creature is the *first* and the *last*, and he who says, HE is himself the *first* and *last*, testifies also, that he is THE ALMIGHTY. Our argument, then, from these declarations may be seen in the following syllogism.

The first and the last is ALMIGHTY.

JESUS CHRIST is the first and the last;

Therefore, *Jesus Christ* is ALMIGHTY.

But it may be said, that "there are two persons who declare themselves to be *first* and *last.*" If that is admitted, *these two* persons must be *one in essence* or in nature, or we have *two* Almighty Beings, which makes two Gods; and the FIRST and the LAST expressly says, that there is no God beside himself. How much better it would be for Unitarians to confess what Christ himself says, that He and his Father are *one*, than to be driven to the unavoidable extremity of admitting *two* beings to be *God*, or two Gods. There are either two *Almighty Gods*, or Jesus Christ, in his divine nature, is one with the Father, or *He and his Father are one.* "And they cease not day nor night, saying; Holy! Holy! Holy! Lord God Almighty, which was, and is, and is to come." Rev. 4:8. Verse 11. "For thou hast *created* all things." Here:

The Creator of all things, is the *Lord God Almighty.*

Jesus Christ is the Creator of all things:

Therefore, Jesus Christ is the LORD GOD ALMIGHTY.

Admitting he has but *one* nature, this could not

be true; that is, it could not be true of his *human nature.* Says an apostle, " Ye are complete in him, which is the head of all principality and power." Col. 2:10. If Jesus Christ is the *head of* ALL principality and POWER, he possesses *all power.* Here he is represented as not only standing at the head of all power, but of all principality. This conveys the same idea, as that " by him all things consist." Col. 1:17. A few brief remarks may show the evidence of the omnipotence of our blessed Lord.

1. Creation is the work of Omnipotence alone. Creation signifies the production of *being,* where no being existed prior to such creation. The source of all created existence is the *self-moving energy* of an *unoriginated, infinite, unlimited,* and *eternal cause;* and that cause was evidently Jesus Christ in his *divine* nature.

2. The Creator is *necessarily* the *first cause;* and in respect to all his works he must have exercised *his own* creative *energy, not through a creature,* for no creature existed. As he was the *only* being that then existed, he must have made all things *for himself,* and *by himself;* and this the Bible most unequivocally affirms of our Lord Jesus Christ.

3. The works of creation could not have been performed, *officially,* or by *delegated* power, because creative power is the sole attribute of Omnipotence. If all *things* were created by *delegated power,* there must have been *one* who delegated that power, and *another* who received it; and this proves

there were *two* beings in existence before the creation of any; and of course *they* were self-existent,
and consequently two self-existent Gods. Again,
He that received the power delegated, could not
have *had it before*, consequently he was not *God;*
and he who delegated it must have ceased to possess it, consequently he *ceased* to be God. This
scheme of Unitarians, then, must amount to this.
The *infinite*, eternal God, ceases to be God; and a
finite being—a *creature*—immediately becomes such.
Again, if Jesus Christ created the worlds by delegated power, he did not make them for *himself*, but
for him who delegated and employed him. This
contradicts plain declarations of Scripture, which
say, that " *All things* were made BY Him and FOR
Him."

4. " Before the mountains were brought forth,"
there must have been an *infinite* duration, in which
there was no *creature* in existence; and it is evident that all the existence there could have been
was underived and unoriginated, consequently the
omnipotent Creator was all the existence there was
possibly in the universe. Now, we are expressly
told that Jesus Christ " is *before all things;*" therefore the apostle considered him God. There is,
then, the same evidence that Jesus Christ is omnipotent, that there is that he is the Creator of all
things; and there is the same evidence of his omnipotence, that there is of any Creator, or any God.
Christians may confide in this Almighty Deliverer
and Redeemer, who has conquered death, sin, hell

and the devil, and has the keys of death and hell; and into whose hands is placed all power in heaven and earth. He can open and no man shuts; and He can shut and none opens.

While we are considering the character of God our Savior, it would be well to mark his condescension for us, " For though he was rich, he became poor, that we through his poverty might be rich." It would have been condescension in an angel; but while we reflect that it was the Christ, Creator of all things, that suffered while inhabiting a body like ours, we may sink at his feet in humble contrition. The blessed Savior died for us.

> " Who nought deserved, who nought deserved but death,
>   Saving the vilest ! Saving me ! O love
>   Divine. O Savior God ! O Lamb once slain !
>   At thought of thee, thy love, thy flowing blood,
>   All thoughts decay, all things remembered, fade ;
>   All hopes return ; all actions done by men
>   Or angels, disappear, absorbed and lost."

The texts we have cited prove the omnipotence of the Lord Jesus Christ, as clearly as words can express it, for his own mouth declares that he is the *Almighty*.

(1.) He is called the mighty God, and the mighty God is the Almighty.

(2.) The Almighty distinguishes himself from all his creatures by the appellations FIRST and LAST, which *was* and which *is*.

(3.) Jesus says He is the *first* and the *last*.

(4.) These terms convey the same sense when

applied to the Lord Jesus, that they do when applied to Jehovah.

(5.) Jesus Christ, in his divine nature, is the Almighty God, or there are *two* Almighty Gods, which
is absurd. Can a *creature* be proved to be the Almighty God? Certainly not. But we trust the
candid reader will very readily see that Jesus
Christ is called *Almighty.*

CHAPTER IX.

The equality of our Lord Jesus Christ with God the Father.

WE do not pretend that the humanity of our blessed Lord was equal with God the Father, in power and eternity. Trinitarians do not say that the *human nature* of Christ was " the very and eternal God," nor that there are *three* Gods, though frequently accused of such sentiments by their opposers. When we speak of Jesus Christ as being God, we speak of him in his *divine nature.* And when we speak of him as man, we speak of him in his humanity. Now this manner of speaking is in common use. Says David: "Why art thou cast down, O my soul." Here he seems to address his spirit. Again he says, " My flesh and my heart faileth," so we see him mentally speaking of his body, and yet none supposes David was inconsistent in his expression, and in fact this is the every day expression of almost all persons.

But if the Bible speaks of Christ as equal with God, he is so, or the Bible is not true.   " Who being in the form of God, thought it not *robbery to be* EQUAL WITH GOD." Phil. 2:15. No man nor angel can be said to be *equal with* God. But our Lord thought it not robbery (arpagmon) to be so.   The original word (arpagmon,) which is translated " robbery," signifies *seizing by force.* If he had *not been* equal with God, it would have been

"seizing by force" for him to have claimed equality, but there was no robbery in his claiming that
which belonged to him. But the reader will indulge
us in making a few remarks on these words.

1. Jesus Christ was *eternally* in the bosom of the
Father, and of the same dazzling glory with him.
2. He clothed his brightness in a human body.
While he was *transfigured* on the mount before
three of his disciples, he displayed some of his former glory, that glory he had with the Father before
the world was. 3. We see that if he had not been
equal with God, his pretensions to equality must
have been not only robbery but blasphemy. 4. If
he possessed but *one* nature, and *that* was derived,
or created nature, he could not in any sense have
been "equal with God," for the highest grade of
creatures falls infinitely short of equality with God.
5. To be equal with God, is to be God, or there
are *two Gods*, which none will allow. 6. In order
for Christ to have been *equal with God*, he must
have possessed equal power, and equal eternity of
existence, for how, (with any respect to truth,)
could the pen of inspiration call a *creature*, whose
very *existence* was given to him by his Creator,
equal with him? Yet, notwithstanding his glory
with his Father before time began, or creature was
formed, he—

> " Is led by choice to take his gloomy walk,
> Beneath Death's dreary, silent cyprus shade,
> Unpierced by vanity's fantastic ray,
> To read his monuments, to weigh his dust,
> Visit his vaults and dwell among the tombs."

Again: Jehovah says that He is his equal.
" Awake, O sword, against my shepherd, and the
man that is my fellow, (equal,) saith the Lord."
Zech. 13:7. " Therefore the Jews sought the more
to kill him, because he had not only broken the
Sabbath, but said also that God was his Father,
making himself equal with God. " Then answered
Jesus, and said unto them, Verily, verily, I say unto you, the Son can do nothing of himself, but what
he seeth the Father do, for what thing soever He doeth, these also doeth the Son likewise. . . For
as the Father raiseth up the dead, and quickeneth
them, even so the Son quickeneth *whom he will.*"
John 5:18—21. The Jews understood our Savior
right, when they said he made himself equal with
God; for he conveyed the obvious idea that they,
(that is, the Father and Son,) possess the same nature. The Jews accused him of *two* crimes; one
was breaking the Sabbath, the other was making
him the equal of God. We learn from what our
Lord said at this time, that—1. God does no works
but what Christ also does. 2. The Son can do
nothing but what he sees the Father do, consequently if the Son has sinned, the Father also has sinned. If the Son has broken the Sabbath, the Father has broken it also. 3. That such was the
union of nature and design between them, that one
did nothing without the other, and what either did
was equally the work of both. The text in
Zechariah, which we have just cited, proves this
equality beyond the possibility of confutation.

"The man that is my fellow," (Heb. ve-al geber amiti.) The hero that is with me. Here inspiration acknowledges the equality between the Father and Son. Again. Jesus says, "He that hath seen me hath seen the Father." John 14:9. These words our Lord addressed to Philip, when he wished ed Christ to show them the Father. He seemed to possess the same feeling that Moses did when he said, "I beseech thee show me thy glory." Exod. 33:18. He was not with the three apostles to whom the transfiguration was exhibited, and therefore was in some degree, at least, excusable for making this request. What *angel* could in truth say to Philip, *" If you have seen me, you have seen God?"* Was Jesus trying to *deceive* Philip and the rest of the disciples? Certainly not. How could they understand him to be a *creature* when he said this? He also told them that he was in the Father and the Father in him, and the very works that he did, the *Father that dwelt in him really performed.* " I *and my* FATHER are ONE." John 10:30. Could any created being truly say, "I and God Almighty are *One?"* Certainly no one would answer this affirmatively. Well, Jesus did say this, and we must acknowledge him to have been correct. With these unequivocal declarations of inspiration before us, how can we deny that the Lord Jesus, in his divine nature, was *equal* with the Father? And if he possessed but *one* nature, and that derived, must we not unavoidably suspect his veracity! " Let God be true and every man a liar."—*Paul.* How

supremely irreverent it would be for us to call in
question the veracity of him whose garments are
unsullied, whose throne is unspotted, whose mes-
sengers are the holy angels, whose palace is the
heavens, and who hurls the thunderbolts of God,
and guides the lightnings in their vivid march.
With what trembling awe should we receive *all* his
precious instructions, and humbly sit at his feet, and
devoutly implore the guidance of his Spirit.

CHAPTER X.

Jesus Christ, in his divine nature, is God.

As we have before stated, so we say again: if Jesus Christ possessed but one nature, that must have been derived or underived, created or uncreated. If he possessed but one nature, and that was *created*, it would be blasphemy to call him God, in the sense that we call Jehovah *God*. We have already, in Chapter iii., as we humbly conceive, proved that Jesus Christ is an object of *divine worship*, and this is now urged as an evidence of his supreme divinity. Indeed, it seems almost unaccountable, that any one who has read the *second commandment*, can bow down and worship a being whom at the same time he acknowledges to be a *creature!* This would be idolatry. But we see that the worship of Christ is placed in direct opposition to the worship of idols. 1 Cor. 8:4—6.

It is evident that the same things which in the Old Testament are ascribed to *Jehovah*, are, in the New Testament, ascribed to our Lord and Savior Jesus Christ. We add only a few.

Isa. 6:5—10.

"Then said I wo is me! for I am undone, because I am a man of unclean lips, for mine eyes have seen the King, the LORD OF HOSTS.

John 12:37—41.

"But though he had done so many miracles before them, yet they believed not on him, that the saying of Esaias the prophet might be fulfilled, which

Then flew one of the seraphims unto me, having a live coal in his hand, which he had taken with the tongs from off the altar. And he laid it upon my mouth, and said, Lo! this hath touched thy lips, and thine iniquity is taken away, and thy sin purged. Also, I heard the voice of the Lord, saying unto me, Whom shall I send, and who will go for us? Then said I, here am I, send me. And he said, Go and tell this people, Hear ye indeed, but understand not; and see ye indeed, but perceive not. Make the heart of this people fat, and make their ears heavy, and shut their eyes; lest they see with their eyes, and hear with their ears, and understand with their heart, and convert and be healed."

he spake:—Lord, who hath believed our report? and to whom hath the arm of the Lord been revealed? Therefore they could not believe, because that Esaias said again, He hath blinded their eyes and hardened their heart, that they should not see with their eyes, nor understand with their heart, and be converted, and I should heal them. These things said Esaias when he saw his glory and spake of him."

Ps. 78:56.

" Yet they tempted and provoked the *most high* GOD, and kept not HIS *testimonies.*"

1 Cor. 10:9.

" Neither let us tempt CHRIST, as some of them also tempted, and were destroyed of serpents."

We see, from these passages, that the Preserver, Director, and Controller of all things, to whom the Old Testament writers ascribe the name GOD, is called *Christ* in the New Testament.

But as further proof of the supreme divinity of our Savior, we will transcribe the testimony of John, "In the beginning was the Word, and the Word was with God, and the Word was God. The same was in the beginning with God. All things were made by him, and without him was not any thing made that was made." John 1:1—3. Verse 10. "And the world was made by him." It is evident that before there was any creation, all was eternity. When creation was not begun, *all* that then existed was certainly *self-existent*. *Self-existence* implies *eternal* existence. John speaks in the manner in which Moses spake when he said, "In the beginning God created." "In the beginning," (En arche,) seems to carry our minds back as far as our finite capacities can extend, and at that time (if we may thus speak,) this "*Word*," (*Logos*,) existed. Was he an *attribute* of God? Was he only the *reason* of God? or was he truly God, as John testifies. This *Logos* was either a *real existence* or he was not. If it is said that this "Word" was only the *wisdom* of God, or an *attribute* of Jehovah, how can it be said that *one* of the attributes of God "*became flesh, and dwelt among us?*" And why is not some of the other attributes of God personified? Admitting the *Logos* to have been an *attribute* of God, there could certainly be no reason for say-

6

ing that "he was with God," for the attributes of
all beings are with them. There never, perhaps,
was any one, who held that the " power" of God
was not with him. But mark—John does not only
say that the "*Logos*" was with God, but that he
was God. But, to use the words of another, in part,
it is difficult for us to divine how he could say, that
any attribute, (*power* or *wisdom*,) *was* God, understanding the word "God" in any sense whatever.
If it means *supreme God,* then it reduces itself to
this; either that one attribute is the supreme God,
or there as many Gods as attributes. If it mean
an *inferior* God, then the *wisdom* of God, being an
inferior God, implies that the other attributes are
superior Gods; or else that his wisdom holds the
place of *quasi* God,* while his other attributes oc-
cupy a lower place. Again: if it is said that the
Logos or *Wisdom* does not signify an *attribute* of
God, but his *essence,* how could it be called ' *Theos,*" for the divine essence is called, *Theiotes. Theos,* (God,) implies an *agent* or *person,* and not the
essence of a person. Now, is an express revelation
necessary to teach us that the *attributes of God
are with God?* or what can be thought of the assertion, that the *wisdom* or *power of God* is God
himself. But " the *Logos was with God*"—all
agree with God the Father. Was not, then, the *Logos,* who was with God, *diverse from that God
with whom he was,* at least in some sense? It was
the same being who became *incarnate,* and was in

* Almost, near upon.

some respect diverse from the Father, and therefore not to be confounded with him, consequently
he was not an *essence, nor* yet an *attribute* of God.
" *And the Logos was God.*" If, as some aver,
the Logos is the *wisdom* of God, and not in any-
wise distinct from the Father, it involves the depths
of mystecism to say that he *was God.* What would
be thought, should a man gravely assert that the
wisdom of a man was the man himself? John
plainly informs us that while the *Logos* was God,
(*Theos,*) at the same time there was a sense in
which he was *with* God. In order, then, that the
words of John can have any possible meaning, a
distinction in the Godhead, must, we think, unavoidably be admitted; that is, that the Father in all
respects, is not the same as the Son. But what
could be the object of John in asserting that the
Logos was *with God?* We answer, to indicate
conjunction, familiarity, and *society.*

Thus far, we see that the evidence of the supreme
divinity of our Lord is conclusive. Christ is called the
Lord of Hosts. "Sanctify the Lord of Hosts himself,
and let him be your fear, and let him be your dread.
And he shall be for a sanctuary; but for a stone of
stumbling, and for a rock of offence," &c. Isa. 8:
13, 14. This prophecy was fulfilled and applied by
the spirit of inspiration to Christ our Savior. 1 Pet.
2:4. It is altogether unnecessary to swell the number of quotations; for, if the texts brought are rele-
vant to the subject of discussion, they are enough
to sustain the proposition, that Christ in his divine

nature is the supreme God. We will only add a
few more. "To the only *wise God* our *Savior*, be
glory and majesty, dominion and power, both now
and ever." Jude, 21 verse. "Of whom, as concerning the *flesh*, Christ came, who is over ALL,
God blessed forever." Rom. 9:5. "*As* concerning *the flesh*," *to kaia sarka.* This has respect to
his human nature, as may be readily proved by consulting corresponding passages. Rom. 1:3. Acts
2:30. "*Who is over all,* God blessed *forever,
Amen.*" *Ho on epi panton Theos eulogetos eis tous
aionas. Amen.* This is properly translated, "Who
is *supreme God* blessed forever." Nor is there
different sense conveyed when we say, "*supreme
God*," and when we read more literally, "*over*
ALL God." Is there any God infinitely above
him who is styled, *epi panton Theos?* Certainly
this phrase means nothing but *supreme God.* It is
clear from this text that Christ, in some sense, de-
scended from the Father, (that is, in respect to his
human nature,) and that at the same time he was in
some sense, (that is, in his divine nature,) *over all*
God, or *supreme* God. "Thy throne, O God, is
forever and ever." This the apostle affirms was
said to the SON. "But unto the Son he saith."
Heb. 1:8. "And we know that the Son of God is
come, and hath given us an understanding, that we
may know him that is true; and we are in him that
is true, even in his Son Jesus Christ. This is the
true God and eternal life." 1 John 5:20. There
can be no doubt that John refers to Christ when he

says, "This is the true God and *eternal life.*" He
frequently applies the appellation, LIFE, and
ETERNAL LIFE, to Christ. "In him, (Christ,)
was LIFE, the LIFE was the light of men—giving LIFE to the world." "For the *Life* was manifested and we have seen it, and bear witness, and
show unto you that ETERNAL LIFE, which was
with the Father, and was manifested unto us." 1
John 1:2. John nowhere calls the Father, "the
life," ETERNAL *life*, and so we must conclude
that he calls Jesus Christ the "*True God*," and indeed why should he not, when he had previously
said "*the Word* was GOD." But, without multi-
plying proof on this point, we refer this proposition
to the candid reader, and inquire: Is not Jesus
Christ called God in the New Testament, in such
a sense, that there can be no doubt that the *supreme
God is certainly intended?* If Jesus Christ is what
HE and the holy apostles say he is, he should be
revered as such. It is not safe to trifle with his holy character, or try to *drag* him down among created beings and things. We shall "See the *Eternal* Judge descending," and hear his awful voice,
and stand before his dread tribunal. God grant
that we may be prepared for that solemn scene.

CHAPTER XI.

*There is a Plurality of Persons in the God-
head.*

WE use the words *"persons in the Godhead,"*
only to convey an idea directly opposite to that
doctrine which asserts that the Son is a being, created or produced by the Father, infinitely distinct,
(being only a creature,) and that the Holy Spirit is
only an *emanation*, attribute, or power, of the Father, and in no sense distinct from him. We do
not use the term *" persons,"* when applied to God,
to denote separate and distinct existence in the being of God; but we apply it to the term *Godhead,*
in order to convey the idea that the *essence of God*
is *known to us* as Father, Son, and Holy Spirit, and
that the Son is not a creature, but truly God, and
the Holy Spirit is not a " power," or " energy," of
the Father, but that he, also, is truly God. It is
evident that a *distinction* in the *Godhead* exists, but
it is equally evident that we cannot define that distinction by the term *persons,* so as to convey the
idea we intend, without giving the sense in which
we use the term. By *person,* then, we mean *"that
which can design."* It is not denied by Unitarians,
that in this, or any sense of this term, the Son is a
person. This is admitted on all hands. Then it
only remains for us to prove that the Holy Spirit is
a *person,* and not an *attribute* of another person.
The reader will bear in mind, that this proposition,

viz. *That the Spirit is an agent*, a *designer*, and not a power, or an attribute of the Father, is the *fulcrum* on which the whole matter now rests, and on which it turns. Why, then, do we conclude that the Holy Spirit is a *person*, and not a power of another person?

1. " The Scriptures ascribe to the Holy Ghost the ACTS and *attributes* of an intelligent being. He is said to guide, (John 16:13,)—to know, (1 Cor. 2:11,)—to move, (Gen. 1:2,)—to give information, (Acts 10:19,)—to command, (Acts 13:2,)—to forbid, (Acts 16:6,)—to send forth, (Acts 13:4,)—to reprove, (John 16:8,)—and to be sinned against, (Mat. 12:32.)

2. The attributes of God are applied to the Holy Ghost; such as *eternity*, (Heb. 9:14,)—omnipresence, (Ps. 139:7,)—omniscience, (1 Cor. 2:10, 11,)—Goodness and *truth*, (Neh. 9:20. John 14:17.)

3. The works of God are ascribed to the Holy Ghost. Creation, (Job 26:13,)—inspiration, (2 Pet. 1:21,)—giving of life and sanctification, (1 Pet. 3:18. 1 Cor. 6:11.)

Now, reader, can you think that the Holy Spirit is a *mere* attribute or *power*, or emanation of the Father? Will you not say he is an *agent*, a *designer*? If so, this is all we wished to prove, for Unitarians do not contend that the Holy Ghost was ever created. It has been, and can be, as readily proved that the Holy Spirit *designs*, as that there is a Holy Spirit at all. Now, what folly it would be to assert that there is design, and yet no *designer*, or that HE who designs is no *agent*—no *intelligent being*, and no *person*. This, with all its absurdity, is the inevitable and unavoidable result of denying the *personality* of the Holy Ghost. How our soul recoils at the thought of stripping the Holy Spirit of design, and intention, and personality. Love to the Holy Comforter would prompt us to say:

> " Hail God the FATHER, heavenly light ;
> Hail CHRIST the SON, my soul's delight ;
> Hail HOLY GHOST, come dwell with me,
> Through time and in eternity."

There is *abundant* evidence of a distinction in the Godhead, and we ask, if Father, Son, and Holy Ghost, do not constitute this *divine* essence, denominated " *Godhead*," what does constitute it?

But if the Holy Ghost is only an attribute, how with any degree of propriety could he be said to be *sinned* against? " *Were the Holy Ghost only an attribute of God, this unpardonable sin could not be committed against him. For, though man can sin against an individual, he cannot sin against one of his attributes, abstractly considered.*"—(*Treatise, p.* 49.) This distinction in the Godhead, which we wish to make, by use of the term " *person*," then, is one that never leads us as *Trinitarians* to the acknowledgement of more than *one God.* It is admitted, and positively declared, in the creeds of Trinitarians, that there is, *numerically* but ONE God. Why, then, should our Unitarian

friends endeavor to force upon our meaning of the
term, the unwarranted idea that we *do mean* by
"*person*" when applied to the divine Being, to convey the idea of more Gods than one? We repel
the assertion. Again. The plurality of *persons* or
hypostases in the Godhead is proved by the use that
the pen of inspiration has made of the supreme
name—the noun and pronoun. Gen. 1:26. "Let
us make man." Gen. 3:22. "The man has become like *one* of *us*." This the "Lord God" says,
"And the *Lord God* said, "Behold the man is
become as ONE OF US." How could this expression of Jehovah have been made, if there is no
distinction in the Godhead? Gen. 11:7. "Let US
go down, and there confound their language?" Isa.
6:8. "Also I heard the voice of the Lord saying,
Whom shall *I* send and who will go for US." Indeed in the very first verse of the Hebrew Bible
this *plurality* in the Godhead is brought to
view. Yes, in the first mention that is made of
the Supreme Being. "The original word *Elohim*,
God, is certainly the plural from *el*, and has long
been supposed by the most eminently learned and
pious men, to imply a *plurality* of *persons* in the
divine nature. As this plurality appears in so many
parts of the sacred writings, to be confined to *three*
persons, hence the doctrine of the TRINITY,
which has formed a part of the creed of all those
who have been deemed sound in the faith from the
earliest ages of Christianity. Nor are the *Christians* singular in receiving this doctrine, and in de-

riving it from the first words of Divine Revelation.
An eminent Jewish rabbin, Simeon ben Joachi, in
his comment on the sixth section of Leviticus, has
these remarkable words: "Come and see the mystery of the word Elohim: there are *three degrees*
and each degree by itself *alone,* and yet notwithstanding they are all *one* and *joined together* in *one,*
and are not divided from each other." He must be
strangely prejudiced indeed who cannot see that the
doctrine of a Trinity, and of a Trinity in Unity, is
clearly expressed in the above words."* The phrase
" *Bara* Elohim," " *the God's created,*" occurs more
than *thirty* times in the short history of the creation. The phrase JEHOVAH ELOHIM, " *the
Lord Gods,*" occurs at least *one hundred and thirty* times in the law of Moses.† " Go ye," says the
blessed Jesus, "teach all nations, baptizing them in
the name of the *Father* and of the *Son* and of the
Holy Ghost." Mat. 28:19. It may be well to remark again, that it is a more literal translation, to
read, instead of baptizing them " *in* the name," " *into* the name," as the preposition (*eis*) *into* is used
in the original and not the preposition (*en*) in. This
does, we think, not mean, " by *the authority*" but
into a recognition of the Father, Son, and Holy
Ghost as the Supreme God.‡ This it appears was
the acknowledgment of those who were baptized.

* See Clarke on Genesis 1:1.

. † See Tomlin's Theology and Hebrew Bible.

‡ See Chap. III. of this work.

Be this, however, as it may, there was evidently a
distinction made between the Father and the Son
in this commission, and also between them both and
the Holy Ghost. Unitarians will admit the distinction between the Father and Son, but not between
the Father and the Holy Ghost. But admitting, as
Unitarians say, that the Holy Spirit is only a " power," or " attribute," of the Father, and that the Son
is a *creature* " neither self-existent nor eternal,"
and we must read the commission, " Go ye into all
the world and preach the Gospel to every creature,"
(mark,) " baptizing them in the name of the Supreme God, and in the name of a finite creature,
and in the name of a *power* or attribute of the Supreme God. And this last name would be mere
tautology, for when an individual is baptized in the
name of the Father, this embraces *all his* attributes, and then to call the name of *one* of these
attributes over the candidate would be only tautology. But to pretend that the Son and Holy Spirit should be associated with the Supreme God in
this solemn act, while there did exist such an infinite disparity, one being only a creature, the other
an *attribute* of the Father who had just been named, discovers almost impervious darkness of mind,
or a determined obstinacy and self-will. Says the
word of inspiration, " The grace of our Lord Jesus Christ, the love of God, and the communion of
the Holy Ghost, be with you all." 2 Cor. 13:14.
Will it here be denied that the Father is a *person?*
Will it be contended that the Son is not a person—

not an agent? No, we presume not by any one.
But was the *Holy Ghost* a *person*, or an agent?
This then is the question we wish to settle, and we
think it will soon be settled in the mind of every
candid reader, that there is the same evidence of
the personality of the Holy Spirit, that there is of
the Son, or the Father. Did Paul invoke the blessing of the *Supreme God*, and of a *creature* and of
an attribute of the Supreme God, to rest upon these
saints? When Christ was baptized in the Jordan—
the Father, speaking from heaven, and the Holy
Spirit descending like a dove, and lighting upon
him, was there no proof of the personality of the
Holy Spirit? And when the body of our Savior
is divinely said to have been conceived by the
Holy Ghost, is there no evidence that the *Holy
Spirit* was a *person, an agent?* We most solemnly
conceive, that the reason that some see no evidence
of the personality of the Holy Ghost, is because
they will not see it. If then the personality of the
Holy Spirit is sustained, the Unitarian notion that
HE is only a "power" falls, and all the appendages
of this notion must fall with it. We will soon conclude this chapter, after most devoutly saying with
Dr. Watts—

"Come *Holy* Spirit, heavenly Dove,
    With all thy quick'ning powers,
Come shed abroad a Savior's love,
    And that shall kindle ours."

Again, in proof of the personality of the *Holy*
Spirit, we will only remark, that the *Holy* Spirit is

represented as having a *mind.* "And he that searcheth the hearts knoweth what is the *mind* of the SPIRIT, because HE maketh intercession for the saints according to the will of God." Rom. 8: 27. Here we have it expressly declared, that he that searches the hearts knows *what is the* MIND OF THE SPIRIT. Here is an active, efficient agent brought to view, possessed of a *mind* and called the *Spirit.* This proves his personality beyond a doubt, if we doubt not the personality of the Father. It also shows a distinction between the Holy Spirit and the Father, and this we term personality, because we can find no word that will better convey the idea we wish to convey, than the word "*person.*" We do not pretend to be competent to fathom the *manner of this distinction* in the Godhead, any more than we do to comprehend the uncreated existence of Jehovah, yet we admit it as a fact firmly based on the authority of Divine Revelation.

CHAPTER XII.

The Number of Persons in the Godhead are Three.

In proof of this position, we shall show that the same *attributes* and *works* are applied to the Father, Son, and Holy Spirit, and that these attributes and works are those which belong to God alone.

1. Eternity. *Father.* "The eternal God is thy refuge." Deut. 33:27. Isa. 40:28.

Son. "Before *all* things." "The beginning and the end." Col. 1:17. Rev. 1:8.

Spirit. "Through the eternal Spirit." Heb. 9: 14.

2. Omnipresence. *Father.* "Do not I fill heaven and earth, saith the Lord." Jer. 23:24.

Son. "The Son of Man which is in heaven." John 3:13.

Spirit. "Whither shall I fly from thy Spirit." Ps. 139:7.

3. Infinite knowledge. *Father.* "Thou only knowest the *hearts* of all the children of men." 1 Kings 8:39.

Son. "He knew all men . . . . what was in man." "Thou Lord which knowest the hearts." John 2:24. Acts 1:24.

Spirit. The Spirit searcheth all things, yea, the deep things of God. 1 Cor. 2:10.

4. Almighty power. *Father.* "Power belong-

eth unto God." " Thine is the kingdom, the *power*, and the glory." Ps. 62:11. Mat. 6:13.

Son. Christ the *power* of God and the wisdom of God." " All *power* in heaven and earth is given into my hands." 1 Cor.1:24. Mat. 28:18.

Spirit. " Abound in hope through the power of the Holy Ghost." Rom. 15:13. " By the power of the Spirit of God." Verse 19.

5. Creation. *Father.* " Hast thou not heard, hast thou not known that the everlasting God, the Lord,* the Creator of the ends of the earth, fainteth not, neither is weary." Isa. 40:28.

Son. " By him were all things created which are in heaven and in earth, visible and invisible." Col. 1:16.

Spirit. "The Spirit of God hath made me." Job 33:4.

6. Each of these persons inhabits the same temple. *Father.* " Ye are the temple of the living God. God hath said I will dwell in them and walk in them." 2 Cor. 6:16.

Son. " That Christ may dwell in your hearts through faith: Christ is in you except you be reprobates." Eph. 3:17. 2 Cor. 13:5.

Spirit. Your body is the temple of the Holy Ghost." 1 Cor. 6:19, and 13:13.

7. Each person possesses, and gives life.† *Father.*

* Here the Creator seems to be spoken of in the person of the Father.

† No being possesses life inherently, and of himself, but God.

" The Lord thy God, he is thy life." Deut. 30: 20.

Son. " He that hath the Son, hath life. In him was life." " This is the true God and eternal life." John 5:12, 1:3. 1 John 5:20.

Spirit. " The Spirit is life." Rom. 8:10.

8. Each is said to raise the dead. *Father.* " God quickeneth the dead." Rom. 4:17.

Son. " The Son quickeneth whom HE will." John 5:21. "I have power to lay down my life and to take it again." John 10:18. " Destroy this temple, and in three days *I will raise* it up." John 2:19. " He raised Lazarus, a daughter, and a widow's son."

Spirit. " It is the Spirit that *quickeneth.*" John 6:63. "Jesus Christ quickened by the Spirit." 1 Pet. 3:18.

We may add, that from the Old Testament we have abundant proof of a plurality of *persons* in the Godhead, and in the New Testament, we find the number limited to *three.* This is evident from the doxologies to Father, Son, and Holy Ghost, and as we have already seen from the baptismal formula.

We would ask, in view of the *attributes* and *works,* which are ascribed by the word of inspiration to the Father, Son, and Holy Spirit, if there is not a *distinction* in the Godhead? We are aware that this distinction is clearly sustained, and that it is not a distinction of the attributes of *one person,* but that each of these distinctions has attributes which

constitute them *persons, agents,* or *designers.* This
being settled, we find the distinction is limited to
three persons denominated in Scripture, FATHER,
SON and HOLY GHOST. The attributes ascribed to these persons, are the attributes of God and
none else. The attribute *eternity* of existence,
none save God can possess. *Omnipresence* cannot
be the attribute of any *creature,* or thing. The
power to *impart life* and resuscitate the dead, be-
longs inherently, as we have proved, to each of the
persons, and consequently they are *all agents* and
designers. We do not enter into proof of these
last statements, for it is self-evident that such attributes as *Eternity* and Omnipresence belong to God
alone, and that these *powers* and attributes must
constitute the possessor an intelligent agent, and
consequently a *person.* How devoutly, then, should
we regard the name of the " Sacred *Three,*" who
co-operate in the scheme of man's salvation, in
such perfect oneness.

"To God the Father's throne,
    Perpetual honors raise,
Glory to God the Son,
    To God the Spirit praise.

With *all* our powers,
    Eternal King,
Thy name we sing,
    While faith adores."

CHAPTER XIII.

The Father, Son, and Holy Spirit, are one God.

TRINITARIANS are often accused of holding sentiments, which involve the idea of " *three* self-existent and eternal Gods." This assertion is not fairly
made, because we do not, in the distinction we
make in the Godhead, by the term " *persons*" wish
to convey, nor *do* we convey, the idea of *three* distinct Gods, and it is certainly unfair and illiberal to
force a meaning upon our language, in respect to
this subject, while we positively assert that such is
not the sense in which we use the term. In the
sense in which we use the term *persons*, no idea of
a *plurality* of Gods is involved. While we assert
the *trinity* of *persons* in the Godhead, we also believe in the *unity* of God. In all the confessions of
faith among Trinitarians on this point, there is but
one idea, and that is " *there is but one* God." We
have now before us the testimony of *eleven* or *twelve*
Trinitarian creeds on this point, and their united
declaration is, " There is but *one* God." But in
what does this *oneness* of God consist? We say it
consists of *three* distinctions in the Godhead, known
to us by the appellations, Father, Son, and Holy
Ghost, and in order to distinguish them from mere
attributes as one *person* or agent, we use the term
" *person*," and apply that term to each of them.
We ask any candid man if this is an acknowledgment of three Gods. The word *trinity*, in itself,

conveys the idea we wish to convey. It will be remembered that this word is composed of the two
Latin numerals, *tres* and *unus*. *Tres* signifies
three, and *unus one*, and it is saying *three in one*.
"How can three be one, and one three?" "In no
way we necessarily and cheerfully reply." "How
then is the doctrine of Trinity in Unity to be vindi-
cated?" In a manner that is not at all embarrassed
by these questions. " *We do not maintain that the
Godhead is three in the same respects that it is one*,
but the *reverse*." Our Lord Jesus Christ is God,
as we view the subject, *only in connection with the
Father*, and Holy Spirit, and so we believe in respect to the Father and the Holy Spirit. The
three distinctions in the Godhead, termed by us *persons*, are one in essence, and *eternity*, and but *one*
God. But to the law and the testimony. "Now there
are divers *gifts*, but the same Spirit, and there are
differences of administrations but the *same Lord*,
and there are diversities of *operations* but the *same
God worketh* ALL in *all*." 1 Cor. 12:4—6. "I
and my Father are *one*." John 14:3. "He
that hath seen me hath seen the Father." John 14:
9. " For there are three that bare record in heav-
en, the Father, the Word, and the Holy Ghost, and
these *three are* ONE." 1 John 5:7. In the *first*
text we have just quoted, we find that *gifts* are at-
tributed to the *Spirit*, *Administrations* to the Lord
Jesus Christ, and *Operations* to God the Father,
and yet it is said that the " *same God* worketh *all
in all*." It will still be borne in mind that Unitari-

ans agree that the Father and Holy Ghost are one, and Jesus says: "I and my FATHER are ONE. We think we need not multiply proofs that the essence of God, or the Godhead, is known to us in three distinctions, denominated in the Holy Word, Father, Son, and Holy Ghost, and that "these *three* are *one*." And now

> "To Father, Son, and Holy Ghost,
> One God whom we adore,
> Be glory as it was, is now,
> And shall be evermore."

CHAPTER XIV.

Consequences of the doctrine which teaches that Jesus Christ is not truly God, and truly man.

WHILE we state the logical result of the Unitarian system, we hope that our deductions may be fairly made. We aim to have them just, and we trust the reader will be convinced that this is our intention. But how dark is the picture before us!

1. If Jesus Christ is not truly God, he was not the promised Messiah. The promised Messiah was one "*whose goings forth were from old, even from everlasting.*" Micah 5:2. "His name shall be called Wonderful Counsellor, The Mighty God, The Everlasting Father, The Prince of Peace." Isa. 9:6. If He was not God, in his divine nature, how could his "goings forth" have been from *everlasting?* and how could he have been the Mighty God, the Everlasting Father?* He

---

* The reader is referred to a note on the words, " Everlasting Father" in chapter xvii. of this work. We hope Trinitarians will be careful never to confound the personality of the Father with that of the Son. Great injury is done to the cause of truth by taking this course. Some of the hymns of Trinitarians are to be repudiated on this ground. We will mention one or two.

"Well might the sun in darkness hide,
And shut his glory in,
When God the mighty Maker died,
For man the creature's sin."

Christ, in his *divine nature*, created the worlds, but in his human nature he suffered, to atone for our sins. The essence of God can

could not have been thus described. Then the proph-
ecies respecting him are not fulfilled, and consequently he is not the promised Messiah.

2. The Mosaic dispensation is not abrogated, but
is in full force and virtue. "The sceptre shall not
depart from Judah, nor a lawgiver from between
his feet, until Shiloh come, and unto him shall the
gathering of the people be." Gen. 49:10.

3. The Jews were not to blame for putting him
to death for blasphemy. "Art thou the Christ?
Tell us. And he said unto them, If I tell you, ye
will not believe, and if I also ask you, ye will not
answer me, nor let me go. Hereafter shall the Son
of man sit on the right hand of the POWER of
God. Then said they all, Art thou the Son of
God? And he said unto them, ye say that I am.
And they said, What need we any further witness?
for we ourselves have heard of his own mouth."
Luke 22:67—71. For this they crucified him. "Be-

neither bleed nor die. It would be better to sing :—

"When Christ the mighty Savior died."

We will copy another verse of the same kind.

"O love divine, what hast thou done,
   The immortal God has died for me,
The Father's co-eternal Son
   Bore all my sins upon the tree;
The immortal God for me hath died,
   My Lord, my Love, is crucified."

Now, the sentiment of this verse is not only incorrect, but it is
absurd. Immortal, means undying; and to say immortal life ceased—that that which could not die, *did die,* is absurd. The dullest
intellect can see this.

cause he being man maketh himself God," for he
said "I am the Son of God." If he was in no sense
God, then his execution was just and according to
their law, for he made himself God, which would
have been blasphemy.

4. No atonement for sin is made. If he was a
creature, he could only do his own duty, and consequently could have done nothing to set to our ac-
count, nor restore that which he took not away.

5. Christ was a vile deceiver and impostor. He
told Philip that he that had seen him, had seen his
Father also. He also stated to Nicodemus that
while he talked with him, he was at that moment
"*in heaven.*"

6. The New Testament is a cunningly devised
fable. If Jesus Christ was "all divine," he had
no blood to shed, nor could divinity die and rise
from the grave. So our faith in Jesus Christ is
vain, and the holy apostles are false witnesses, for
they testified he rose from the dead.

7. The Christian religion is a deception, for God
was not manifested in the flesh, in the person of
the blessed Savior.

8. The most pious Christians on earth are gross
idolaters. They have always "called upon the
name of the Lord Jesus Christ," and worshiped
him, as the Supreme Deity.

9. All who worship Jesus Christ as God, will
unavoidably be lost, for we are commanded to worship none but God.

10. The true Messiah is yet to come.

11. Judaism is true.

12. Deism is correct.

13. Mohammedanism is preferable to Christianity. Mohammed charged the Christians with idolatry because they worshiped Jesus Christ, which he considered the unpardonable sin. Says he, " Surely God will not pardon the giving him an *equal.* Verily God will not pardon the giving him a companion, but he will pardon any crime besides that." *Kor. Vol. ii. p.* 104. Again he says, " When ye encounter unbelievers, strike off their heads . . . . kill *idolaters* wherever you find them." Voltaire, Mohammed, and all the infidel world, have tried to destroy the worship rendered to Jesus Christ. Voltaire's most blasphemous watchword was, " *ecrasez l' infame ;*" that is, "crush the wretch," meaning Jesus Christ. If Jesus Christ is not God, his worship is idolatry, and the Koran is true instead of the Bible. Mohammedans, Atheists, and Deists, all ridicule the doctrine of the Trinity, and are all in sentiment Unitarians. We grant that a person may be a Unitarian and not be a Deist, but he cannot be a Deist unless he is a Unitarian. And we heartily believe that there are some misguided Christians that embrace this deadly doctrine, but we can see no middle ground between Trinitarianism and naked Deism.

We now ask the reader: Are not the above inferences purely logical? If they are, the doctrine of Unitarianism is death to Christianity. Dark indeed is the system, and its tendency is to sap the very foundation of every *true believer's* hopes of walking the paradise of God. It is a blow at the root of all revealed religion.

14. The tendency of Unitarianism is, to the disbelief of the sacred word of God. In proof on this point we will copy a report of a sermon, delivered in Boston at the recent ordination of the Rev. Charles C. Shackford, by the Rev. Theodore Parker of Spring Street, Roxbury. It was reported by J. H. Fairchild, pastor of Philips church, Thos. Driver, pastor of South Bap. church, and Z. B. C. Dunham, pastor of 5th M. E. church, Boston, May 28, 1841.

We copy the caption prefixed by the editor of the Morning Star.

"Unitarianism. Christians will read the following with feelings of regret and pain. It shows the downward tendency of Unitarianism, and the importance of maintaining sound doctrine and wholesome discipline."

Sermon. Text—*Heaven and earth shall pass away, but my words shall not pass away.*

"It has been assumed that every word of the Scriptures was inspired, with all their vulgarities, absurdities, and impieties. Men have appealed to the Old Testament, as authority, and condemned some of the most pious and devoted, as infidels, because they could not believe all which is written in it as inspired, where there is much, never, perhaps, designed to be taken as truth. Thus questions have been settled by the authority of the Old Testament. It has been assumed that the Old Testament, in all its parts was inspired, and men have

8

been stigmatized as heretics and infidels, who would not give up their reason and humanity to the belief of the story of Abraham and his son, as of divine origin, a story which is revolting to justice and humanity.

The same has been assumed of the New Testament, the obvious contradictions and absurdities of which are everywhere apparent; and which contains stories the most incredible and sometimes shocking to decency. And yet this book is declared to be the word of God and given by divine inspiration! What apostle ever pretended that this book was divinely inspired? Did Jesus Christ ever assume that he spoke by divine inspiration?

The great body of Christian professors make their doctrines rest on the authority of Jesus Christ, and not on pure Christianity.

Real Christianity-life was *out* of the church, and in the world, for the first *four* centuries.

Doctrines have nothing to do with a man's Christianity.

Christianity would have lost nothing by the perishing of the Old Testament or the New. And if different individuals should arrive at different results, and even opposite results, still, this will not affect their Christianity, or authorize the withholding of Christian fellowship.

Christianity is true, but all systems of Christians are false.

Because some pious Christians have cut off the end of John's gospel, and the beginning of Matthew's, they have been branded as infidels.

Christianity does not rest on the opinions of a few pious fishermen, or on the New Testament.

Christianity was the same *nineteen* centures before Christ, as *nineteen* centuries after Christ.

The Bible is not our master or despot. We may take the Prophets as our teachers, but we must not bow down to their idol notions.

The Bible does not tell us that God exhausted his capabilities in creating Jesus Christ. We may yet expect men, as gifted and elevated, or, even more so, as Christianity is hereafter unfolded.

We are not saved by Christ who lived nineteen centuries ago, but by the Christ that we find in our own hearts. If it could be proved that Christ never lived, or that he was an impostor, still Christianity would not be affected by it! So, if the apostles had never lived, or were impostors, Christianity would still be the same. It was taught by nature.

Christianity has no creed, or, if it has a creed, it is a creed of only one article, viz. that there is a God.

Christianity must be tried by the oracle in the human heart.

We want no one to stand between us and God. If we would have the full benefits of a spiritual Christianity, we must worship the Father as Jesus did, with no intervening mediator and then we shall be like Christ."

Here we have Infidelity—daring, bloated, unvarnished Infidelity, preached at an ordination, by a professed minister of the gospel, under the curtains and coverings of Unitarianism. Such men in the sacred desk! Wolves in sheep's clothing!! Now, we ask the candid reader, Does not Unitarianism tend to the disbelief of God's holy word? and were we incorrect when we stated that there was no middle ground in our view, between *Trinitarianism* and *Deism*? Satan, the old red dragon, when the church was in its infancy, clad himself in his crimson garb, and dyed it deeper still in the Martyr's blood. But when the church became more numerous, he laid aside his blood-stained dress, and

clothed himself in white, or " transformed himself
into an angel of light," and we need not marvel that
his ministers should do the same.

CHAPTER XV.

The Statements and Doctrine of Unitarians.

THERE are a number of classes or societies, who agree in the Unitarian doctrine, while they disagree in many other matters of faith. Some of these societies take the name *Unitarian*, or *Congregational Unitarian*. Others call themselves *Christians*, and we are informed by a very respectable member of the *Universalist* society, that they also are Unitarians.

It is a very difficult matter to state what Unitarians *believe* respecting Jesus Christ and the Holy Ghost, for they do not seem to agree among themselves, yet it is easy to see what they *do not believe*. The Unitarians have formerly existed under the names of *Arians*, *Sabellians* and *Socinians*. The *Arians* were the followers of Arius, who was a presbyter of the church of Alexandria about the year 315. "Arius maintained that the Son of God was totally and essentially distinct from the Father; that he was the first and noblest of those beings whom God had created—the instrument by whose subordinate operations he formed the universe. He also held that the Son was inferior to the Father, both in nature and dignity, that the Holy Ghost was not God, but created by the power of the Son." His views respecting the Son seem to harmonize perfectly with the views of modern Unitarians, but they, perhaps, differ in respect to the nature of the

Holy Spirit. The *Sabellians* were "the followers of *Sabellias*, a philosopher of Egypt, who flourished in the third century. The *Sabellians* held that there was but *one* person in the Godhead—that the Word and Holy Spirit are only virtues, emanations, or functions of the deity; that the Father of all things was born of the Virgin, that he diffused himself on the apostles in tongues of fire, and was then denominated the *Holy* Ghost."

That there is *but one person* in the Godhead, is the belief of modern Unitarians. So here they agree with the ancient Sabellians. Also, do they seem to agree that the Holy Ghost is only an emanation of the Father, but further they seem not to agree.

The *Socinians* were so called from *Faustus Socinus*, who died in Poland in 1604. They maintain "that Jesus Christ was a mere man, who had no existence before he was conceived by the Virgin Mary, that the Holy Ghost is no distinct person, but that the Father is truly and properly God."

With this, modern Socinians, or Unitarians, will not fully agree. They agree, or seem to agree, that only the Father is properly God, and that the Holy Ghost is in no sense a person, or distinct from the Father. They seem to disagree in this; that Jesus Christ did exist before his nativity; but yet they deny that his existence was eternal, and unequivocally affirm that "Jesus Christ is not eternal." We will now attend more particularly to the statements of modern Unitarians.

Says a modern Unitarian,* while speaking of what Christ *is not*:—"He is not *unoriginated*, he is not *self-existent*, not *immortal*, not *unchangeable*, not *omniscient*, not *all-wise*, not *all-good*, not *all-powerful*, he is not *omnipresent*."

We now have it fairly stated what Christ *is not*, and these statements leave us to infer after all, what he really is, in view of Unitarians.

Says the same writer, "Christ possesses but *one* nature." "The two nature doctrine," he says, "is essentially incredible, a palpable contradiction." "The doctrine of the two natures, implicates the moral character of the Holy Jesus."†

Again he says, "Christ testifies that he is not God." "Jesus *denies* being God—denies calling himself God, and repels the accusation of blasphemy, even on the supposition he *had* called himself God."‡

Again, "The Father is the *only true* God." "Trinitarians professedly worship two other objects beside the Father." "I see not how they can claim the character of 'True worshipers.'"‖

* The Unitarian just named, is Mr. Morgridge. The above is found in his "True Believers' Defence," page 50. Mr. Morgridge is a minister of the *Christian* denomination. He seems to have possessed a peculiar faculty for disposing of those texts which deal death to his system, for when there was no other way for him to clear his system from collision with the positive declarations of Jehovah, he pronounced them "*spurious*," with all the boldness of a Bolinbroke.

† See Morgridge's "True Believers' Defence," page 70.

‡ See page 44 of the above-named work.

‖ See page 40. Query. Does he not mean to convey the idea

From the above, it is clear what *modern Unitari
ans* think Christ *is not*, but it is not stated what he
is.

Says another Unitarian writer, while trying to
prove that Christ was not omniscient: "Of that
day and hour knoweth no man." "This," says
he, "would embrace his human nature, if he had
one; and then what? Why, he now *rises* to *angels*,
no, *not the angels*, and from an angel he rises high-
er still, and says, *neither the Son.* This certainly
embraces his *highest nature*, above angels, and yet
the Son in his highest nature, did not know when
the day of judgment would be."[*]

Says another, "The power or wisdom of God
was made flesh, a little above *our* flesh, a little
above *human* flesh." " The flesh came down from

that Jesus Christ is not an object of religious worship? and if
those who worship him are not true worshipers, are they not *idolaters?*

* The writer of this extract is Elder Oliver Barr, a minister of
the *Christian* denomination, formerly of Sinclearsville, N. York.
The pamphlet from which we copy is entitled, " *Truth Triumphant,*" p. 14. It seems that with all his sagacity he did not discover
that he flatly contradicted the Bible. "But we see Jesus, who was
made a little lower than the angels for the suffering of death,
crowned with glory and honor." Heb. 2:9. Now, if he possessed
but one nature, it must have been *that* nature which St. Paul meant,
when he said, he was made a *little lower than the angels.* Elder
Barr thinks that the Lord Jesus *rises* from angels to *himself*, but on
the hypothesis that he possesses only *one* nature, he *falls* down
from angels to himself, or the text we have quoted is false. But
there is one way to avoid any collision with *inspiration.* Just get
Mr. Morgridge to pronounce it " *spurious!*"

heaven and became poor." "That which died on the cross, *human* or *divine*, call it which you please, is worshiped in heaven." "We worship *two* beings, the Father and the Son." "The Holy Ghost is not a person at all, but is a power of the Father and a good power."[*]

We might multiply statements to show where these negative assertions place the blessed Savior, but the foregoing we think may suffice. From these statements, we wish to draw our conclusions in accordance with their nature and designs; and in this way we hope to ascertain the certainty or fallacy of the doctrine. We shall therefore devote the subsequent chapter to plain, logical deductions from the testimony and statements of modern Unitarians respecting their own views of the character of our Lord Jesus Christ.

[*] These are the statements of Elder Badger of the *Christian* denomination, made at Parma, N. York, in his discussion with the writer. Mr. Badger was formerly *editor* of the " *Palladium*."

9

CHAPTER XVI.

Plain Logical Deductions from the Statements of modern Unitarians.

In the following conclusions and deductions, we shall endeavor to draw such inferences as the sense most obviously dictates. We have no design to make deductions foreign from the design of the authors we have cited, knowing if we do we shall be contending with a " man of straw."

1. Says one of the authors quoted, " Jesus Christ is not *unoriginated*." From this we conclude *he must have had an origin,* and there must have been a time when his origin took place, consequently there was a time when he was not originated, and of course when he did not exist. The Bible gives us the origin of his body, that is, his human nature; and if that was all the nature he possessed, he did not exist before the worlds were made.

2. " Not self-existent." If he is not self-existent, his existence must have been caused by some being, and that being gave him existence, consequently he is not the Creator, but is in every sense a creature, and if so, is unworthy of acts of religious worship.

3. "Not immortal." The being who is not immortal must be *mortal.* This is as evident as the axiom that " whatever is, is." That being that is mortal is subject to death. Then the deduction is, *Jesus Christ our Savior may die!* Man has one

immortal nature, and if Jesus Christ possesses *but one* nature, and that is mortal, he is far below man.

4. " Not invisible." Trinitarians do not pretend that the body of our Savior is invisible, but He says, "Where two or three are assembled in my name, there am I in the midst of them." Certainly his body is not in the midst of every little group of saints, and it is equally certain that his children know his presence to be invisible. Jesus Christ " was God, manifested in the flesh," and we cannot divine how a *visible* being can fill heaven and earth with his presence at the same time. John 3:13.

5. " Not unchangeable." We understand that Jesus Christ is the same yesterday, to-day, and forever. Heb. 13:8. (See chapter vii. page 24.)

6. " Not omniscient." If this is correct, he has to learn things beyond the reach of his senses, by means of *foreign instruction*. This is making him like one of us, who only know what we are told, or what we learn from books. This would render him very incompetent to judge the world, or say "depart from me, ye workers of iniquity," for his lack of omniscient knowledge, might lead him to err in judgment. And in fact, it would disqualify him for knowing the desires and prayers of his dear children here in the world.

7. " Not all-wise." Then he may be deceived, and led astray. If he is not all-wise, he *must* be ignorant, at least in some degree. Jude calls him, " The only *Wise* God, our SAVIOR."

8. " Not all good!" How shocking is that sentiment. What blasphemy and irreverence of his sacred character! If this sentiment be correct, there must be *faults* or *wickedness* attached to him.

9. "Not all-powerful." There are, then, many things beyond his power. He says he is the first and the last, the ALMIGHTY. He is said to be the "wisdom of God, and the power of God." If this is true, his power may fail in the accomplishment of his designs, if he has *wisdom* to design.

10. " Not omnipresent." If our Lord Jesus Christ is not omnipresent, he is totally unable to fulfill his engagement to be with his disciples always even unto the end of the world. He could not be a much better Savior than Baal, when his prophets prophesied, and cried, " O Baal, *hear* us."

We now see by these negative attributes, where Unitarians place Jesus Christ. Where is the man of whom the same might not be said, that here is said of the adorable Savior? A being who had his *origin* lately,* whose *existence* depends on another: who is *mortal, changeable*—and in some respect not good, the Savior of this ruined world! Who could trust such a being with an *immortal soul*, in a day of trial and danger? Who could call on his name for help, in a dying hour, and say, " Lord Jesus, receive my spirit?" Who could trust the inter-

* There is an infinite remove, in duration of existence, between the origin of any being that has had an origin, and the self-existent and Eternal God.

ests of an undying soul to one who had, perhaps,
only *wisdom* sufficient to manage his own con-
cerns?

It is the obvious deduction from each, and *all* the
foregoing statements, that Jesus Christ is viewed
by modern Unitarians as a *mere creature*, in all respects a finite being, the production of creative
power—that his worshipers are not *true* worshipers—that his worship is idolatry—that he is incompetent to be our Mediator—and unworthy of our
worship or our praise; and when compared to the
Eternal Being, he appears as a mere *ephemera*. The
very moment he is robbed of infinite *power*, *wisdom*, and goodness, he is reduced to a creature.
What reasoning this. May God deliver his children from this snare, this stratagem of Satan. Soon
the writers of the above statements will know
whether Jesus Christ is omniscient or not—whether he is possessed of the wisdom of the immutable
God, or not, and whether he is all good or otherwise. The coming day will reveal the character of
our Lord Jesus Christ.

CHAPTER XVII.

Some of the most Prominent Objections to the doc-
trine of the Trinity, considered.

1. Says Mr. Morgridge, "The doctrine of the
Trinity is to be rejected, because the belief of
it is *impossible.*" If this objection is correct, if it
can be shown to be impossible for a man to believe
the doctrine of the Trinity, in the sense and light
in which Trinitarians hold it, then the consequences are these:—*First,* Unitarians are under no ob-
ligation to believe it. *Second,* it is not true. *Third,*
Trinitarians *do* not believe it. *Fourth,* those who
pretend to believe it, are all false witnesses, and li-
ars. *Fifth,* Trinitarians are all hypocrites, or they
would abandon it. *Sixth,* no man on earth does,
or ever did, believe it. But where is this impossi-
bility? It might be impossible for us to believe as
Unitarians *represent* the doctrine of the Trinity.
But as we *hold* it, there is no difficulty in believing
it. Jesus Christ says, " I and my Father are one."
" He that hath seen me, hath seen the Father."
Unitarians admit the Father and Holy Ghost to be
one, and all they lack is to believe what Christ says,
and then the matter is at rest. So the item that
they esteem impossible to believe, lies between them
and the Savior, and he says, " except ye believe
that I am He, ye shall die in your sins."

2. Says the same writer, "There is no passage
of Scripture, that asserts that God is *three.*" We

think there are a number. Not that say, however, that there are three Gods, but that bring
to view in the character of God *three distinctions,*
which we denominate *persons.* "The grace of
our Lord Jesus Christ, (*one,*) the love of God,
(*two,*) and the communion of the Holy Ghost,
(*three,*) be with you." "In the name of the *Father,* (*one,*) and of the *Son,* (*two,*) and of the *Holy Ghost,*" (*three.*) "Come ye near, I have not
spoken in secret from the beginning, from the time
that it was, there am I, (*one,*) and now the Lord
God, (*two,*) and his Spirit, (*three,*) hath sent me."
Isa. 48:16.

3. "Trinitarians," says Mr. Morgridge, "professedly worship two other objects beside the Father." He thinks the Son is not to be worshiped
as God. "Ye cannot serve (Gr. *Douleuein*) God
and mammon." Mat. 6:24. "Ye serve (Gr. *dou-
leuete,*) the Lord Christ." Col. 3:24. Here the
same word denoting *service* is applied to God and
to Christ. Christ informed satan that it was written that God *alone* should be served, and his followers *served* the LORD Christ. They were either
idolaters, or they considered Christ Lord of all.

Again. "Thou shalt worship (*proskuneseis*)
the Lord thy God." "And they worshiped him,"
(Christ) *proskunesantes,* &c. Luke 24:56. Here
the same word, and one that conveys the idea of
the *same kind* of worship, is applied to the Father,
and also to the Son. Now are we to be considered *idolaters* because we also worship the LORD

CHRIST? Where Christ speaks of the "true worshipers," he says they shall worship (Gr. *proskunesousi*,) the Father in *Spirit*. It was the manner of the worship he here speaks of. It was to be *spiritual* worship. He did not teach, that true worshipers should not worship the Son too in Spirit, but he taught men to "Honor the Son, even as they honor the Father."

4. "Jesus denies being God, he denies calling himself God, and repels the accusation of blasphemy, even on the supposition he *had* called himself God."[*]

The same author on this point goes on to state, that Jesus did convince the Jews that they were wrong in charging him with blasphemy, and thus satisfied their minds. Now these statements are *utterly incorrect*. He did not deny making himself God. The Jews did not ask him if he was God, but they asked him if he was *the Christ*. John 10:24. He calls himself the Son of God, and testifies that he and his Father are one. We repeat it. He did not deny making himself God, after he was accused by the Jews, but *repeated* his former statement. John 10:38. The writer then states that the Jews were satisfied that he did not intend to be understood, as making himself God. They were *not* satisfied, and as they went to take him, he made his escape. John 10:39. It was for this very sentiment, that he was condemned at the

[*] See True Believer's Defence, page 44.

judgment seat of Caiaphas. Here he was accused
of professing to be the Christ, and Caiaphas said to
him, " *I adjure thee* by the *living God, that thou
tell us whether thou be the Christ, the Son of God.*"
Then, under the solemnities of an oath, Jesus answers him *affirmatively*, and says, " *thou hast said.*"
" Nevertheless I say unto you, Hereafter shall ye
see the Son of man sitting on the right hand of
power, and coming in the clouds of heaven." Mat.
26:63—64.

Does this look as though he " repelled the accusation?"* Not at all; for on this acknowledgement
he was condemned.

We have already stated in chapter ix. that the
Jews understood the Savior correctly. This is evident from the fact that they considered him guilty
of blasphemy. Had they understood him, (as Unitarians do,) as only professing unity of *sentiment*
and *design*, with the Father, they would not have
accused him of blasphemy, for Moses, Elijah, and
David, professed as much as that. He did not say
he and his Father " were *one* in the business of
watching the sheep," as Mr. Morgridge says he intended. But he professed an *unity of nature* with
his Father.

* When we read these statements of Mr. Morgridge, a professed
minister of Christ, we were shocked. When he states that " *Christ*
satisfied the Jews that He did not pretend to make himself God,"
we could but suspect not only the piety, but the veracity of the man.
The reader will find these quotations on page 44, and the following
pages, of his work.

Now we ask ; Did Jesus Christ decline the appellation, GOD? Did he deny being GOD? Not at all. But when one of his disciples looks on him, and says to him, " My Lord and my GOD," he seemed to incur the approbation of the blessed Savior.

Never did he satisfy the Jews that he did not intend to be understood as making himself equal with God.

5. It is stated by Mr. Morgridge and Mr. Barr, as well as other Unitarian writers, that our Lord Jesus is not omniscient, because there was one thing that he said he did not know. Mr. Barr thinks it was the " day of judgment." The text they use to show him not omniscient is as follows. " But of that day and that hour knoweth no man, no, not the angels which are in heaven, neither the Son but the Father." Mark 13:32. Another evangelist has it thus. " But of that day and hour knoweth no man, no, not the angels of heaven, but my Father only." Mat. 24:36. The expressions contained in these texts we acknowledge to be of the same, or nearly the same, import. In Matthew, however, the " Son" is omitted. We will now endeavor to come at the sense of the text quoted from Mark.

Says the Savior to the Pharisees, " Ye judge after the flesh; I judge no man." John 8:15. Again he says, " 'The Father judgeth no man, but hath committed all judgment unto the Son." John 5:22. In the first of these texts, he was asked to pass his

judgment upon a certain woman. He informed
them that that was not his present business. Not
that he had *no power* to judge, for long before this
he had told them that "all judgment was committed to the Son;" but he wished to inform them that
in his present employment he could not judge in
that matter. One thing is clear, he had the power
or ability of knowing that day he spoke of, or he
had not. The "*day* and hour," the Savior spoke
of, was not the "day of judgment;" but he spoke
of the desolation of the Holy City.* All the preceding and attending circumstances he described,
and the result of the day. He told his disciples,
that of the temple, there should not "be left one
stone upon another that should not be thrown down."
He also knew that "her enemies would cast a
trench" around the city. Daniel fixed the year of
the destruction of Jerusalem more than *five hun-*

* 1. It is evident that Christ was here speaking of his coming
again to visit Jerusalem, not in mercy as at present, but in dreadful
vengeance. 2. The text says : " But of that day and that hour."
It only remains to show *what* day and hour he refers to. He says,
verse 33, " Take ye heed, watch and pray, for ye know not when
the time is, for the Son of man is as a man taking a far journey,"
&c. Verse 27, he says " Watch ye, therefore, for ye know not
when the master of the house cometh." It will not be doubted,
that when he speaks of the coming of the *master of the house,* he
means his *own* coming, and he declares, verse 26, that they shall
see the Son of man coming in the clouds, and, verse 30, he says,
" This generation shall not pass away, till all these things be done."
But it does not affect our argument in favor of our Lord's omniscience, to admit that he here had some reference to the final coming of the Son of man at the last day.

hundred years before this. "Seventy weeks are
determined upon thy people, and upon thy holy
city, to finish transgression and make an end of
sins, and to make reconciliation for iniquity, and
to bring everlasting righteousness, and to seal up
the vision and prophecy, and to anoint the MOST
HOLY." Dan. 9:24. It is evident Daniel was informed when it was. Who gave him this information? We answer, "The spirit of Christ." "Of
which salvation the prophets have inquired and
searched diligently, who prophesied of the grace
that should come unto you, searching what or what
manner of time the *Spirit of Christ* which was in
them did signify." 1 Pet. 1:10, 11. Now with
these facts before us shall we conclude that Christ
had not the *power of knowing* when that day should
arrive?

"Knoweth no man," &c. The word, *oiden* is
the 2d *per* of *eido*, "to know," and is variously
rendered. "To know" is its obvious meaning.

But the next question is, in what sense the Savior
used it? "If this passage signifies that the knowledge of Christ was limited, it plainly contradicts
those already quoted, which prove he is omniscient.
But considering the word *know* to have the
same meaning here that it has in 1 Cor. 2:2.
"For I determine not to know any thing among
you, save Jesus Christ and him crucified," it involves no obscurity, for it there has the causative
sense. "I determine not *to cause to know*, or *make*

known."* If Jesus by his spirit gave Daniel information when this should take place *five hundred and seventy* years before this, is it not strange that he had not the power of knowing it, when the event was "nigh, even at the doors?" We think the undoubted sense in which the Savior used the word "to know," was as above stated; for says one, "Hast thou not heard, hast thou not known, that the everlasting God the Lord, the Creator of the ends of the earth, fainteth not, neither is weary? there is no searching of his *understanding*." Isa. 40:28.

6. Mr. Morgridge devotes one chapter of his work to a search for the "supposed second person of the Trinity," and says, "God the Son does not exist," "there is nothing for him to do," and tells us that "God the Son," is the creature of human creeds." He bases his argument mainly on the following passage of holy writ. "Then cometh the end when he shall have delivered up the kingdom to God, even the Father, when he shall have put down all rule and all authority and power; for he must reign till he hath put all enemies under his feet. The last enemy that shall be destroyed is death. For he hath put all things under his feet. But when he saith, All things are put under him, it is manifest that he is excepted that did put all things under him. And when all things shall be sub-

* See the Faith of the F. Baptists, page 44, 45, and the *remarks* there made on Mark 13:32.

dued unto him, then shall the Son also himself be
subject to him that put all things under him, that
God may be all in all." 1 Cor. 15:24—28. " Here,"
says Mr. Morgridge, " We see the same dependent
Son, giving up the kingdom to the Father."

We will make a few brief remarks on this passage.

First.   The kingdom the Son is to give up. The
"end" the apostle spoke of was the end of the
present world, the grand close of human affairs.
Christ during this period acts as our Mediator and
Intercessor, but at the end of the world this office
must cease, there being no more need of a Mediator. It is, then, the Mediatorial kingdom that is
given up.

*Second. To whom the kingdom, or reign, is giv-
en.* It is evident that the reign is given up to the
Father.   But is it to be supposed that the Father
was inert, and had nothing to do with the reign all
this time, and now the Son is to be inactive? Certainly not.   Man's probation being closed, the distinction in the persons of the Holy Trinity, in
atoning for, *sanctifying*, and *pardoning* men, and
preparing them for heaven, now ceases. The divine nature of the Savior being superior to his human nature, is now the all-controlling, all-absorbing
Deity, and now—

> " The God shines gracious through the man,
> And sheds sweet glories on them all."

Third.   Who is all in all.   The apostle informs
us that " God shall be all in all." In Col. 3:11, he

speaks of Christ as being "all in all," but it was on a different occasion from the one under consideration. But mark, he does not say that the *Father* shall be all in all, but GOD shall be all in all. The distinction in the divine essence as now recognized by us will cease, and

GOD be ALL in ALL.

We have abundant evidence that this is the sense of the text, for God says of the Son, "Thy throne, O God, is forever and ever." And the Revelator tells us he saw the "Lamb in the midst of the throne."

Let men make light of the existence of "God the Son," because that nowhere in the scriptures this precise form of expression is used, yet they will find him without much search in a coming day! Jehovah calls him God. "Thy throne, O GOD." Jesus says he that "the SON makes free is free indeed," and therefore we have no scruples in giving him the appellation "God the Son." And now "to the only wise God our Savior, be glory and majesty, dominion, and power, both now and ever." Amen.

7. It is again stated by the last mentioned author, that though Christ is called God, it is in a subordinate sense, and therefore it does not prove him to be the "Supreme God." We have yet to learn that the Christian religion admits of different grades of Gods, Gods superior and inferior. We unhesitatingly state that the term "god," is no where in

the Bible applied to men or angels, unless it is used
in the *plural* number, or preceded by the article *a,*
or otherwise qualified by the sense, so that it *cannot
be understood to mean the Supreme Being.** But
where it is applied to Christ, this distinction ceases
to be made.

Says one, "Christ is not what the Bible
calls him. He is called a Rock, a Lion, a Lamb."

It should be borne in mind that these titles denote
different *characters* under which he is revealed to
us. When spoken of as a sacrifice for our sins, he
is denominated a lamb. When his power and ability "to take the book, and unloose the seals, is spoken of, he is compared to a Lion, and his immutability is spoken of under the figure of a Rock.

But is he inferior to the objects that figuratively
represent him? What is he when he is represented by the terms, "Mighty God," "Everlasting
Father,"† "True God, and Eternal Life," "Great

---

* Mr. Morgridge says, "Moses is called Jehovah, their God."
Deut. 11:13—15, and that "Jonathan calls David, O Lord God of
Israel." 1 Sam. 20:12. See Morgridge's work, page 122 and 125.

What man, and especially what Christian, can but blush at such
statements as these! The reader may consult the sacred text,
Henry's, Clarke's, or any other Commentary on earth, to see how
untrue these statements are. The fact is, *truth* is not now, nor
ever will be, indebted to falsehood for its support. But how fruit-
less must be such attempts to destroy the doctrine of the Supreme
Divinity of our blessed Lord. That cause that truth will not sustain, is a bad cause, and should be forthwith abandoned.

† The term, "Everlasting Father," in this passage, we think,
does not refer to the *first person in the Trinity,* but to Christ, as

God," "Only Wise God," "The first and the last, the Almighty?" If he bears, in the sacred Word, such appellations as these, and yet they do not prove his Supreme Divinity, there can be certainly no proof from the word of inspiration, that any Infinite Supreme Being exists in the universe. We would ask, if these titles would prove the Father to be the self-existent God? and if so, what do they prove in relation to our Lord Jesus Christ?

But the time of vain speculations on the character of Christ will close ere long; that day when God the Son shall take the throne of judgment and call all human beings before his face. *Our* eyes will *see* him clad in robes of judgment. We shall see those flaming eyes and burning feet. Our ears will hear his pleasing voice, bid us welcome to the mansions of unsullied bliss, prepared eternal in the heavens; or we shall tremble at that voice which says, "*depart.*" Our hearts will flutter in our bosoms, filled with joy; or sink within us, convulsed with awful terror. Then will shine forth the attributes of him who was dead, and is alive, and has the keys of death and hell. Forbid it, blessed Jesus, that we should be deceived!

the Author, Creator, Governor, and Protector of the Universe, or the Father of all created things, and of the Gospel dispensation. Trinitarians should be careful not to confound the idea of these two persons. Let the distinction always be maintained.

10

QUESTIONS ON THE CHARACTER OF CHRIST.

We will subjoin the following, and give the answers as far as we can, in accordance with the views of modern Unitarians. Those we do not answer, we shall leave for any Unitarian to answer, who is better skilled in the mysticisms of that doctrine than we are at present. But until these questions are answered in agreement with the views of Unitarians, we shall consider them *unanswerable.*

QUESTIONS.

1. Did Christ exist *before* his nativity? A. Yes.

2. Is his existence eternal? A. No.

3. Is Christ *all* divine? A. Yes.

4. Can Divinity die? A.

5. Was there ever any *incarnation* of the divine Being? A. No.

6. How was God manifested in the flesh? A.

7. Is the Son an object of religious worship? A. Yes.

8. Is any *creature* an object of religious worship? A.

9. Did the body of Christ exist previous to his conception and birth? A.

10. Was that body *human, angelic,* or divine in its *nature?* A. Divine.

11. Can Divinity bleed? A.

12. Had the actual Creator any partner in creating the universe? A. No.

13. Who was the Creator? A. *Christ.*

14. Did the body of Christ possess a human soul? A. No.

15. Was it the body or mind of Christ that created the universe? A.

16. Is the Holy Ghost an active agent, a person? A. No.

17. How then was the Holy Ghost, the Father of Jesus Christ? A.

18. Was the Creator of the universe a *separate* and *distinct being*, from him who died on the cross? A.

19. Was the Creator himself uncreated? A. Yes, he was.

20. Was Jesus Christ self-existent? A. No.

21. Did Jesus increase in wisdom? A. Yes.

22. Did the Creator increase in wisdom? A.

23. Did Jesus Christ possess *two natures?* A. No.

24. In what sense was Jesus before Abraham? A.

25. Is there any *created* being who was from everlasting to everlasting? A.

26. Is any created being the *living* God? A. No.

27. Why is Christ so called? Acts. 14, 15. A.

28. Is the Eternal God a spirit? A. Yes.

29. Is a spirit a mind, an agent, a person? A. Yes.

30. Is the Holy Ghost a person? A.

31. Is the Holy Spirit and the Spirit of God, one, and only one, Spirit? A.

32. How is God said to be a Spirit? A.

33. Does Christ possess *human nature*? A. No.

34. Why is he called " Jesus Christ of the seed of David?" A.

35. Was the God of Elijah, Jeremiah, and Daniel, the Eternal God? A. Yes.

36. Why does Jesus call himself, " The Lord God of the Holy Prophets?" Rev. 22:6—16. A.

37. Was the Logos, (John 1:1,) a real existence? A.

38. Was he a substance, or was he an attribute of God? A. An attribute.

39. Was the world created by delegated power? A. Yes.

40. Can God delegate his attributes? A.

CONCLUSION.

It is with feelings of devout regard and veneration for the Supreme Being, that we have approached the subject we have been contemplating in the preceding pages. We make no pretensions to any ability to *comprehend* the uncreated existence of the Infinite and Holy ONE. All such pretensions, we esteem folly and blasphemy.

It may not be improper to say, that some who are Trinitarians, *nominally*, carry their views so far as to give up the doctrine entirely, and take the ground they most strenuously oppose; and, in fact, are in sentiment Unitarians. The moment we deny the *distinction* between the Father and the Son, and assert that they in all respects are the same being, that moment we are on Unitarian ground, with this difference, that they hold thus of the Father.

It matters not whether we consider the Father, Son, or Holy Spirit, the *only* proper Deity. If we lose sight of the *distinctions of persons in the Trinity*, we take the side of Unitarianism, or Socinianism, which differs somewhat from the views of modern Unitarians, as we have already shown. If we declare the Son to be God, to the exclusion of the personality of the Father and Spirit, not acknowledging them at the same time to be God equally with the Son, we overreach the doctrine of the Trinity, and become supporters of the doctrine we oppose. We are represented as holding that "the very and Eternal Father died on the cross," and then we are tauntingly asked, "Who supported the universe while God was dead?" We deny holding any such doctrine. We constantly make the distinction between the persons of the Father, Son, and Holy Ghost. We do not believe that the Eternal God died, but we do believe the human body of the Lord Jesus died, and this is one reason why we believe in the humanity of Christ, for we *cannot believe* that Divinity could bleed and die. We confidently believe our Lord and Savior, in his divine nature, to be God with the Father and Holy Ghost, and therefore we make no distinction in the worship

we render him or them. We do not bow our knees
a little way to Christ, and then bow them down to the
Father, but we bring them *down*, right *down*, at
the name of Jesus Christ. And we do hope, when
this mortal life shall close, to bow with all them
that are sanctified in Christ Jesus, and offer unceas-
ing and undivided praise to GOD, the FATHER,
GOD, the SON, and GOD, the HOLY SPIRIT, in
a world that shall never end.

HYMN.—Praise to God.

Jesus, thy love shall we forget,
  And never bring to mind,
The grace that paid our hopeless debt,
  And bade us pardon find.

CHORUS.

Our sorrows and our sins were laid,
  On thee, alone on thee ;
Thy precious blood our ransom paid,
  Thine all the glory be.

Thy life of grief shall we forget,
  Thy fasting, and thy prayer—
Thy locks, with mountain vapors wet,
  To save us from despair ?

Gethsemane, shall we forget,
  Thy struggling agony,
When night lay dark on Olivet,
  And none to watch but thee ?

Shall we the platted crown forget,
  The buffeting and shame—
When hell thy sinking soul beset,
  And earth reviled thy name ?

The nail, the spear, shall we forget ?
  The agonizing cry ?
My God—my Father, wilt thou let
  Thy Son forsaken die ?

Life's brightest scenes, we may forget,
  Our kindred cease to love,
But he who paid our hopeless debt,
  Our constancy shall prove.

CONTENTS.